GABRIEL GARCÍA MÁRQUEZ

REGINA JANES

GABRIEL GARCÍA MÁRQUEZ

REVOLUTIONS IN WONDERLAND

A LITERARY FRONTIERS EDITION

UNIVERSITY OF MISSOURI PRESS

COLUMBIA & LONDON, 1981

Library of Congress Cataloging in Publication Data

Janes, Regina, 1946–
    Gabriel García Márquez.

    (A Literary frontiers edition)
    1.   García Márquez, Gabriel, 1928–   —Crit-
icism and interpretation.
PQ8180.17.A73Z687   863   80–27286
ISBN 0–8262–0337–X

TO MY MOTHER AND MY FATHER

GABRIEL GARCÍA MÁRQUEZ

I. THE WRITER'S CONTEXT

Rich Oranochy, though but knowen late
Spenser, *Faerie Queene, IV, xi, 21*

In the decade of the 1960s Latin America revealed to herself and to the rest of the world that she had come into her literary golden age. From Mexico, Cuba, Guatemala, Colombia, Peru, Chile, Argentina, Uruguay, Paraguay, and Brazil came poems and novels that crossed national boundaries within Latin America and beyond it.[1] There had been great writers in Latin America before, of course—Sor Juana Inés de la Cruz, Machado de Assis, Rubén Darío—but like Bede's bird flying through the long, lit hall in from the dark out to the dark again, they were birds of passage, solitary illuminations, and not constellations or even a flock, nesting and breeding and staking their territories. In this century, in two generations of writers, that has changed.

Gabriel García Márquez is a member of the second generation of those writers for whom the difficulties that Latin America had presented its novelists became opportunities, and within his generation, he occupies a special place. When, in 1967, after a six-year silence, he published his fourth novel, *One Hundred Years of Solitude* not only became an international best-seller, translated now into twenty-five languages (with the erotic passages censored in the Russian version, the author complained to Pablo Neruda), but it was also acclaimed with unparalleled generosity by the author's peers. Carlos Fuentes, the protean Mexican novelist, hailed the appearance of the novel's first chapters as the discovery of a new world; Julio Cortázar, the Argentine whose *Hopscotch* is one of the most acrobatic literary games since *Tristram Shandy*, took to using García Márquez's example to justify novels like his own that seek to change the world by transforming our imaginative apprehension of it rather than by retelling sad, realistic tales of exploitation and oppression; Guillermo

---

1. The important word is *revealed;* most of the writers who came to prominence in the 1960s had been writing for decades, some for a lifetime.

Cabrera Infante complained that Miriam Gómez, his wife, had not finished his own *Three Trapped Tigers* but had read *One Hundred Years of Solitude* twice. Most remarkably, Mario Vargas Llosa, the Peruvian novelist, eight years younger than García Márquez with several well-received novels to his credit at the time, put himself to work on a massive biographical and critical study of García Márquez, complete with bibliographical apparatus. Something in *One Hundred Years of Solitude* took.

What García Márquez had provided was an inimitable solution to many of the artistic and thematic problems that other Latin American writers had been grappling with in their own very different ways. As he read *One Hundred Years of Solitude* and as he wrote *García Márquez: Historia de un deicidio*, Vargas Llosa was writing a novel that began: "From the doorway of *La Crónica* Santiago looks at the Avenida Tacna without love: cars, uneven and faded buildings, the gaudy skeletons of posters floating in the mist, the gray midday. At what precise moment had Peru fucked itself up?"[2] That opening catches the paradoxical sense that many of its contemporary novelists have of Latin America as a new world gone suddenly old, composed of nations rotten before they were ripe. It also takes on itself the responsibility for that condition: Santiago asks when "Peru fucked itself up," not "who fucked Peru over?"

That skepticism of the national and continental enterprise is a phenomenon of the late nineteenth and twentieth centuries. In social, political, and economic terms, the direction of most Latin American nations after independence was retrograde; after a glorious colonial period in which the cities of the hemisphere most advanced culturally, artistically, and scientifically were all south of the Rio Grande, came independence followed by civil strife, largely unaccompanied by industrial development. As the United States and Europe industrialized, the nations of Latin America remained essentially aristocratic in social structure, with power vested in the control of land and natural resources. Acting as a supplier of raw materials to industrial America and Europe was highly profitable for certain sectors of the population and provided capital for

2. *Conversation in the Cathedral*, trans. Gregory Rabassa (New York: Harper and Row, 1974), p. 3.

2

development in a number of countries, in particular Mexico, Chile, Colombia, Argentina, Brazil, and Peru; but even today there remains a vast discrepancy between the wealth of some and the poverty of many. The political realm is fully as paradoxical: so much rhetoric, so many revolutions, and so little liberty with so many dictators. Such conditions are common in much of the world, but in Latin America they encounter a highly politicized intellectual elite that has long been alive to the conflict between expectations about what politics should be and the actual political and historical experience. The expectations derive from the rationalist, bourgeois, democratic, and socialist traditions of Europe. The actual experience is interminable civil wars, dictators, coups d'etat, brief resurgences of democratic rule, social revolutions promising much and betrayed by the makers of the revolution or aborted by the prompt arrival of the U.S. marines or of CIA funds to finance the counterrevolution. Through all these changes, the language of politics for progressive intellectuals of European culture has been order, progress, democracy, liberty, and later social justice, the revolution, the people. Wherever he looked and wherever he looks, the Latin American writer sees the dance of dictators and the massive exploitation of the poor, all wrapped up in a grandiloquent rhetoric reminiscent of Cortázar's story about the young lady who gave her suitors delectable sugar candies with a cockroach inside.

The literary temptations presented by a continent with such a history, with a topography even more intimidating and extreme than that of the United States and Canada, with large Indian and black populations unassimilated to the European culture of the dominant classes, have overcome novelists of the folkloric or geographic or social realist persuasion from the nineteenth century into the twentieth. What certain contemporary writers have brought to the phenomena is a primary commitment to literature and the imagination that has enabled them to marry the comprehensiveness of scope we associate with the nineteenth-century European novel to experimental forms that recapitulate the paradox perceived at the heart of the Latin American experience. In the first generation, Pablo Neruda ascended the heights of Macchu Picchu and sang a *Canto general* for all of Latin America, for Chile, for himself (and against the United Fruit Company), as Jorge Luis Borges charted the realms of his fantastic metaphysics. In Paris, Miguel Angel Asturias found a double inspiration in surrealism and Mayan myth (and eventually the United Fruit Company), while Alejo Carpentier discovered the duplicities of history and elaborated the critical concept of "lo real maravilloso americano," the "marvelous real," arguing that geographically, historically, and essentially, Latin America was a space marvelous and fantastic enough in its diurnal reality to satisfy any hunger for the fantastic and that to render that reality was to render marvels. In the second generation, in the work of Cortázar, Cabrera Infante, Fuentes, Vargas Llosa, Manuel Puig, and many others, the play with forms began. Novels became "model kits" to be assembled by the reader; parodic entertainments that mingled languages, fragments of plots, and exuberant verbal wit in kaleidoscopic dissolves; or ambitious attempts to render a significant aspect of national history, culture, or identity by fragmenting point of view and the narrative line, illuminating from various perspectives the breaking of men and a society on the wheel of time. Indebted to literature in English from Sterne to Faulkner by way of Dos Passos and Joyce, the writers of the second generation found themselves in still another paradoxical and profitable situation—exploiting the exploiters. In a comic reversal of the imperialist enterprise, they extracted the raw materials of modernist forms, took them back to their own language, and manufactured a multitude of novels to sell in the overdeveloped nations where critics had been mourning the death of the novel. The importance of the variety of formal possibilities opened by modernism can scarcely be overestimated, for that transformation of novelistic convention has enabled modern Latin American writers to manage a wide range of political and social experience without being forced to resolve their fictions by accepting the social order or providential intervention. Instead, the order of fiction can be constructed to resist the present order of things or to reveal it without yielding to any determinism save that of the imagination.

Like many of his contemporaries, García Márquez possesses a double commitment to literature and to social and political change, particularly as such change is embodied in the socialist revolution that triumphed in Cuba in

1959. Vargas Llosa and Cortázar have visited Havana; the preeminently skeptical and detached Carpentier joined the Cuban Communist party and was with the Cuban embassy in Paris before his death in 1980; Cabrera Infante, whose parents founded the Communist party in their Cuban town, worked enthusiastically for the revolution at first, but finally broke with it and installed himself in London, where he carps at Jane Fonda's penchant for protest marches as "'Chic' Guevara." García Márquez worked for the Cuban news agency Prensa Latina from 1959 to 1961, covered the Cuban airlift to Angola in 1976, and has recently completed a book on the experience of the Cuban people under the U.S. blockade. A period of comparative economic prosperity and of new efforts at regional cooperation in the economic sphere, the late 1950s and the 1960s saw a number of political experiments taking hold in Latin America, from leftist triumphs at the polls in Mexico, Santo Domingo, Brazil, and Chile to guerrilla activity in the mountains of Colombia, Venezuela, and Bolivia. Most were quashed in the course of the decade, but it might be argued, cautiously, that the new sense of political possibility, of the imminence of change, freed writers for literature. Gordon Brotherston suggests that the shared commitment to the revolution, both as reality and as idea, has made for a common bond among these writers, impressing on them a stronger sense of themselves as a group with a common artistic and political purpose than they might otherwise have had,[3] and their productions in the seventies certainly suggest a common sensibility, with each writer playing a characteristic variation on a common theme. As Latin America turned into a vast army barracks in the course of the sixties, her novelists in the seventies turned with astonishing unanimity to writing novels on terrorism, military dictators, and military repression: between 1972 and 1976 appeared Carpentier's *Reasons of State*, García Márquez's *The Autumn of the Patriarch*, Cabrera Infante's *View of Dawn in the Tropics*, Cortázar's *A Manual for Manuel*, Puig's *Kiss of the Spider Woman*, Fuentes's *Terra Nostra*.

Writing on political topics is one way to justify the writer's vocation, but there are others that are less confin-

3. *The Emergence of the Latin American Novel* (Cambridge: Cambridge University Press, 1977), p. 3.

ing. When revolution is a serious and desirable possibility, as it is in much of Latin America, the experimental writer of leftist inclinations has to justify himself on several fronts both to himself and to those who attack him—for writing at all, rather than assembling bombs in inconvenient garages, for writing books that do not present themselves immediately as calls to action, for writing difficult books that are not immediately accessible even to those of the people who can read. The commonest defense is that "all good art is revolutionary," that it changes the way readers see and interpret the world, and that through the transformation of the consciousness of readers, by some mysterious means, the world will be transformed. For the most part, that argument can be regarded as an attempt to unify personal desires and convictions leading in different directions in order to justify continuing to do what one wants to do most—to write good books. That these writers themselves find the argument inadequate seems clear when Fuentes and Octavio Paz instigate grass-roots political organizations in Mexico or García Márquez writes on the death of Allende or on Vietnam, serving the revolution not in fiction but in nonfiction. García Márquez has long waffled on the theoretical issue: he has said that a writer's only obligation is to write as well as he can; he has said that he would have done more good had he become a terrorist rather than a novelist, but he has also said that Camilo Torres, the Colombian priest who baptized one of his sons, would have done more good by remaining a revolutionary, communist priest than he did by dying with a band of guerrillas in his first encounter with Colombian troops. That waffling makes good sense, for it makes common sense: writing as a vocation is justified, and fiction is not confused with political action. And the successful writer, who has served a long and solitary apprenticeship to his art, can, as García Márquez and others have, use his influence as an intellectual, gained through the quality of his books, to serve political change. Once the author has gained a usable eminence, he need no longer justify writing: it has justified him.

Although some critics objected that *One Hundred Years of Solitude*, with its emphasis on solitude and its texture of marvels, was a reactionary evasion of issues better treated in *No One Writes to the Colonel* and enjoined the author to return at once to his earlier mode, his fellow novelists recognized in the novel a brilliant evocation of many of their own concerns: a "total novel" that treated Latin America socially, historically, politically, mythically, and epically, that was at once accessible and intricate, lifelike and self-consciously, self-referentially fictive. The relationship to Carpentier's "marvelous real" was immediately evident, and, perhaps most pleasing, the novel was full of allusions to themselves, to Carpentier, Fuentes, Cortázar, Juan Rulfo, and less directly Borges. Ever obliging and always believing in the predictive power of fiction, García Márquez has since discovered allusions to books he had not yet read when, well after the fact, he identified the nun who brings Meme's baby to Fernanda with a character in Vargas Llosa's *The Green House*.

While subjects, aims, and political attitudes may be communal property, books are individual products, their authors solitary entrepreneurs in a labor-intensive industry. García Márquez began, as writers do, with certain topics, obsessions, interests, images that appear in his writing from the earliest works to the latest. These raw materials, the obsession with solitude, nostalgia, and burial alive, the figure of the battered old man, the specter of the civil wars and *la violencia*, have obvious biographical and historical sources. Less obvious is how he learned to transform these materials into the familiar characteristics of his mature style: a richly elaborated and suggestive rhetorical surface, more rococo than baroque, mediated by a single epic voice, and controlled by an intricate and carefully planned, almost diagrammatic structure that ends in perfect, apocalyptic closure. Characteristic of the epic voice is the rendering of character from the outside, externally, just as hyperbole is the characteristic figure of the rhetorical surface. As readers of García Márquez's early work well know, he was not born writing that way. In the early fictions, powerlessness is the essential condition within which his characters live and move, and the world is sad, compounded of losses and hopelessness. Those conditions remain in effect in the later fiction, but in the later fictions García Márquez discovered the transforming power of art, rhetoric, and magic and learned to set against the limitations of human experience the liberating inventions of the imagination. Within the fictions, magical invention does not solve any human problems (indeed, it may cause them), but it alters our relation to and apprehension of them. For the achievement of García Márquez's later fictions is a stylization of his material that permits him to effect an artistic release from reality's limitations while confirming the reader's sense of the reality of those limitations. The danger magical events present to the author tempted by them is that they may become mere wish fulfillment for both author and reader, a fallacious gratification of legitimate desires through escape from the pressures and constraints of the unmagical world in which we live. But García Márquez uses magic to allude to problems in our world, rather than to solve them, and as he turns to revolution for solutions in politics, so he turns to apocalypse for resolutions in fiction.

García Márquez discovered his distinctive tone and apocalyptic closure almost but not quite simultaneously, and both originated in his treatment of political topics. That origin and that simultaneity suggest a fundamental ambivalence toward his material. Formally, the later fictions balance contradictory impulses to destroy and to conserve. Creating artificial universes in which time runs in circles, nostalgia pulls powerfully backward into the past, and episode distracts us from the inevitability of endings, these fictions destroy that fictive, nostalgic, recursive, busy world all at once, once and for all. But an ending, no matter how apocalyptic and thorough, is only a small part of any fiction, which consists principally in that world before it has been done in. García Márquez had treated political topics before he adopted exaggeration, magic, and the impossible; he had treated them severely, bleakly, chastely, as *Innocent Eréndira*, for example, does not. But in his writing from the middle of *Big Mama's Funeral* on, astonishment substitutes for restrained outrage in the narrator's tone, as if something had freed the author from the obligation to treat political topics in a realistic mode or had suggested to him the legitimacy of the exercise of a free imagination that is politically committed, but not bound to the realistic representation of the ills it abhors. While there is abundant literary precedent for such treatment of political topics, in García Márquez's career there is also a striking temporal correlation with the Cuban revolution. The change in style and tone follows directly upon the success of a popular socialist revolution of precisely the kind he

8

had long hoped to see, though he must often have despaired of its probability: a revolution that overthrew a dictator, undertook drastic social and economic changes on behalf of the poorest members of the community, and promised, at least at the beginning, artistic and cultural freedom. García Márquez calls himself a revolutionary socialist, and it might be said that his confidence in the eventual triumph of a socialism that permits the bourgeois liberty of the imagination is as chimerical as levitating with cups of chocolate: neither seems to be occurring in the immediate present, though the one was believed to be possible though miraculous in our cultural past, and the other will seem possible though miraculous when it materializes in our future. But the belief in a future order that is to transcend the present, curing all our social, political, and economic ills, freed him from the internal compulsion and the external obligation to render those ills in a realistic mode, while the belief in the necessity of such a transformation keeps him anchored in our world where those ills are all too apparent.

Since the past to which García Márquez grapples is part biographical, peculiar to him, and part historical, peculiar to Colombia, there follows a biographical and historical note focused, for the convenience of readers, on those details that he has used in his fictions. Most of the biographical information is to be found in Vargas Llosa's *García Márquez: Historia de un deicidio,* a work for which the author had the subject's full cooperation.

A BIOGRAPHICAL AND HISTORICAL NOTE

Born 6 March 1928, a Pisces, in Aracataca, Department of Magdalena, Colombia, a small town a few miles south of Ciénaga (which means "Swamp") on the Caribbean coast in what was then known as "the banana zone," Gabriel José García Márquez was the first of twelve children (including another son named Gabriel and a sister who became a nun) born to Gabriel Eligio García and Luisa Santiago Márquez Iguarán, the town telegraphist who had come to Aracataca in the midst of the "leafstorm" of the banana fever and the daughter of one of the town's leading families, which had strenuously opposed the match. Before the child's birth, with the umbilical cord wrapped around his neck, to which he attributes his claustrophobia, the young couple had removed to Riohacha on the Guajira peninsula, but they returned briefly for the birth, leaving the child with his maternal grandparents until his grandfather's death in 1936.

Almost certainly the original of his grandson's interest in battered old men, Col. Nicolás Márquez Iguarán had married his first cousin Tranquilina Iguarán Cotes and had served under the Liberal Gen. Rafael Uribe Uribe during the War of a Thousand Days (1899–1902), the last of the nineteenth-century civil wars fought between Liberals and Conservatives (called "Goths" by the Liberals). Between independence in 1820 and 1903, sixty-five to eighty civil wars, including a small uprising in 1875 in the Department of Magdalena, mentioned in "Big Mama's Funeral," were fought over constitutional issues, with the Liberals (red their color) favoring a loose federalist structure, universal suffrage, direct elections, limitations on the power of the Church, civil marriage, and freedom of the press, provisions institutionalized in the constitutions written between 1853 and 1863 by the Liberals in power. Conservatives (blue their color) favored a strong central government, supported the Church, and, in their constitution of 1886, denied nationality by birth to the illegitimate children born abroad of Colombian nationals. The War of a Thousand Days, in which Liberals rose against an "Independent" coalition government, was accompanied by particular brutality, for the government refused to recognize the insurgents as belligerents and, by calling them "bandits," as would happen again in *la violencia*, was able to ignore the conventions of gentlemanly war. Such Liberal commanders as Uribe Uribe and Benjamín Herrera, commander of the forces in Panama, called repeatedly for the more humane treatment of prisoners, which was accorded by some Conservative commanders, including Pedro Nel Ospina, with whom Uribe Uribe maintained an affectionate correspondence during the war and through whom he sent messages to his wife. The war on the Atlantic coast was concluded by the Treaty of Neerlandia, where a symbolic tree was planted in the presence of Col. Nicolás Márquez Iguarán. After the war, the colonel and his wife settled in Aracataca, a miniscule town that was to expand rapidly after the First World War with the advent of workers for the banana plantations.

10

When García Márquez was almost a year old, the massacre of the banana strikers memorialized in *One Hundred Years of Solitude* occurred in the railroad station of Ciénaga. In the first decades of the twentieth century in the "banana zone," the United Fruit Company had constructed an irrigation network and maintained its own railroad, telegraph network, retail stores, and fleet to carry its cargoes to U.S. ports. Since the laborers on the banana plantations were not hired directly by the company or by the independent Colombian growers, but were employed by foremen-contractors and migrated from plantation to plantation, both the company and the independent growers were able to evade the provisions of Colombian labor law that required employers to provide workers with medical care, sanitary dwellings, and collective and accident insurance. The workers also objected to payment in scrip redeemable only at company stores stocked with goods from the United States brought in by the returning banana ships. As Miguel Urrutia, a member of the Conservative party, has elegantly put it, "The petition of the workers consisted of nine demands, the principal one being the recognition by the company that it had employees."[4] In 1918, a strike had persuaded the company to agree to consult with its Boston office on the workers' demands; when no results were forthcoming, the workers raised their demands again, ten years later, and another strike began, with widespread support from local shopkeepers and newspapers. The strikers interfered with scabs, stopped trains, and damaged cut fruit. The army was called in, under Gen. Carlos Cortes Vargas, who issued Decree No. 1 on the night of 5 December, ordering the crowd assembled at the Ciénaga train station waiting for the arrival of a promised government mediator to disperse within five minutes or the troops would open fire. Someone in the crowd shouted, "Take your minute!" and the troops opened fire.[5] Accord-

4. *The Development of the Colombian Labor Movement* (New Haven: Yale University Press, 1968), p. 102.

5. Carlos Cortes Vargas, *Los sucesos de las bananeras (Historia de los acontecimientos que se desarrollaron en la zona bananera del Depto. de Magdalena 13 de noviembre de 1928 al 15 de marzo de 1929)* (Bogotá: Editorial La Lúa, 1929), p. 65. García Márquez quotes Cortes Vargas exactly. The further advice in the English version as to what to do with the minute once it is taken is the translator's addition.

ing to Cortes Vargas, there were nine dead; according to Alberto Castrillón, a labor leader sentenced after the strike, 410. The next day, 6 December 1928, Cortes Vargas issued through his secretary, Enrique García Isaza, the Decree No. 4 that declared the strikers a "bunch of hoodlums" and authorized the army to shoot anyone engaged in hostile activities. Estimates of those killed in this "clean-up" operation range from 1,000 to 1,500 with from 2,000 to 3,000 wounded. The army admitted to 200 dead. Jorge Eliécer Gaitán, a radical leader, attacked the army's conduct in Congress, but the event soon fell from view and from the standard secondary-school history text, which mentioned only that public order had been disturbed, but thanks to martial law, tranquillity was restored on 14 March 1929.

Back in his grandparents' house, García Márquez remembers being taken to the circus and shown dromedaries in the dictionary by his grandfather, who also told him, having killed a man in a quarrel in his youth, how heavy the weight of a dead man was. To his grandmother, he attributes the style of *One Hundred Years of Solitude*, for "Whenever she did not want to answer a question, she would invent fantasies so that I wouldn't be saddened by the truth of things."[6] One of her contributions was the Duke of Marlborough: asked who "Mambruck" was in the children's song about "Mambruck's" going off to war, she replied that he had fought in the civil wars with grandfather. Another contribution was sitting him in a corner and telling him not to move or the ghosts would come out of their rooms, in one of which Aunt Petra had died, in another Uncle Lázaro (whose namesake did what the character Melquíades does). An aunt wove her own shroud, said she would die when she finished it, and did; the natural sons of the colonel, born during the war, stayed at the house when they passed through town; a neighboring family claimed that a daughter had not eloped but ascended into the heavens. When his grandfather died, the boy returned to his parents, and his grandmother died in her daughter's house, senile and blind, after the boy had left his parents' home again for high school in Zipaquirá, outside of Bogotá, a high, chilly, gray, misty city where children sleep in the doorways of churches and men sell

6. "The Making of a Classic," *Atlas* (July 1979), p. 50.

lottery tickets on every street corner. Shortly after this removal, when he was about fifteen, he made a visit with his mother to Aracataca to sell his grandparents' house and to encounter the disparity between memory and present reality.

Enrolled as a student in the Faculty of Law at the National University in Bogotá in 1947, García Márquez published his first story in *El Espectador*. That course of study was interrupted and the author's manuscripts destroyed by the *bogotazo* of June 1948, a period of violent riots set off by the assassination of Jorge Eliécer Gaitán, in which, among other buildings, García Márquez's pension burned down. From the *bogotazo* dates the beginning of *la violencia*, an almost twenty-year period of rural violence in which over 200,000 people died at the hands of Liberal and Conservative guerrilla bands, vigilantes, local authorities, and the army. The insurgents were called guerrillas by some, bandits by the government; a few bands were Communist-led; some were secretly supported by leaders of the Liberal party, though repudiated by the national directorate of the party. In 1952, a National Conference of Guerrillas convened to formulate a program including agrarian reform and other radical goals, but the movement remained uncentralized and local, the guerrilla organizations autonomous. In 1953, Rojas Pinilla assumed power in a military coup and attempted, with some but not complete success, to quell the violence. When it flared up again in 1957, he turned power over to the National Front, an agreement between the Liberal and Conservative parties to alternate in power for sixteen years, with a Conservative president one term, a Liberal president the next, and balanced cabinets throughout, an agreement that illuminates the cynical popular saying that "The only difference between liberals and conservatives is that the liberals go to mass at five o'clock and the conservatives at eight." In 1958, the toll of civilian dead reached 300 a month, leveling off at 200 a month for the next four years, until the rate began to fall in 1963. Today, the Colombian government estimates that there are no more than 2,000 guerrillas in the country.

With the closing of the university in Bogotá in 1948, García Márquez enrolled at the university in Cartagena, where his family now lived, once the most important slave

13

port on the Caribbean, with a chain across its bay to keep out marauders. There he wrote for *El Universal*, but he soon gave up the law forever and moved to Barranquilla where he had met "three boys and an old man," all passionate for books. The old man was Ramón Vinyes, a Catalan republican who returned to Catalonia to die; the three boys were Alfonso Fuenmayor, Germán Vargas, and Alvaro Cepeda Samudio, who had been four years old and living in a house that overlooked the square when the massacre took place in Ciénaga and whom García Márquez described in a 1954 review of his first book of short stories as looking like a truck driver.

In Barranquilla, books were supplemented by brothels, including that of the legendary madam, the "Negra Eufemia," and by romance, a discreet passion for the daughter of a local pharmacist, Mercedes Barcha, nicknamed in code for her exotic Egyptian looks, "the sacred crocodile," whom he married in 1958 after extensive peregrinations: in 1954 to Bogotá as a reporter for *El Espectador*; in 1955 to Rome to cover the death of the Pope, who recovered; in 1956 to Paris to starve without a job after Rojas Pinilla closed *El Espectador*; in 1957 to eastern Europe and the Soviet Union, London, and finally Caracas in time to observe the fall of Pérez Jiménez in January 1958. Still working as a journalist, he stayed in Caracas until 1959, when he and his family returned to Bogotá to open the office of Prensa Latina, the Cuban news agency. There his first son, Rodrigo, was born in August and baptized by Camilo Torres, who died in a guerrilla band associated with Victor Medina. A second son, Gonzalo, was born in Mexico in 1962. In 1961, he and his family moved to New York to operate the Prensa Latina office there, resigning in May as a consequence of an internal power struggle over Prensa Latina in Cuba. Traveling to New Orleans through the south and Faulkner country by Greyhound bus, the family intended to return to Colombia, but went instead to Mexico, where García Márquez wrote screenplays, edited two magazines, and worked for the Walter Thompson advertising agency until in 1965, on the road between Mexico City and Acapulco, he "saw" the novel, returned to his house in Mexico City, closed the door in his study, and came out eighteen months later with *One Hundred Years of*

Solitude in his hand to meet his wife with $10,000 worth of bills in hers.

In 1967, after the publication and success of that novel, he made a number of literary appearances and moved to Barcelona where he planned to write *The Autumn of the Patriarch* and did. It appeared in 1975, and the author promptly moved back to Mexico City. He gave the prize money from the Books Abroad/Neustadt International Prize for Literature (awarded in 1972) to a fund for the defense of Chilean political prisoners; founded an organization called Habeas in 1976 to negotiate privately with governments on behalf of political prisoners; and has traveled pen in hand to Cuba, Angola, Vietnam, as well as Sweden, Paris, and Washington, D.C., as a member of the Panamanian delegation to witness the signing of the new Panama Canal treaty. He had to go as a member of the delegation since the United States refuses to grant him a multiple-entry visa under the "ideological exclusion" provision, Section 212(a)(28) of the Immigration and Nationality Act, which denies visas to those who are members of Communist parties and to those who, though not members of any Communist party, as García Márquez is not, may have written or distributed any material "advocating or teaching . . . the economic, international, and governmental doctrines of world Communism." The provision was enacted in 1952.

II. LEARNING A CRAFT

> The Debate [between Truth and Fiction] meerly lies between
> *Things past,* and *Things conceived;* and so the question is only
> this: Whether Things that have Place in the Imagination,
> may not as properly be said to *Exist,* as those that are seated
> in the *Memory;* which may be justly held in the Affirmative,
> and very much to the Advantage of the former, since This is
> acknowledged to be the *Womb* of Things, and the other
> allowed to be no more than the *Grave.*
>
> Swift, A Tale of a Tub, sect. ix

García Márquez published his first short story in 1947 at the age of nineteen; nineteen years later, he was finishing the novel that would make him rich and famous or documented and unhappy, if we are to believe the title he gave in 1974 to a collection of early reportage. In the course of that apprenticeship, he happened on many techniques to which he would later return, invented characters and places he would later develop more fully, and discovered the distinctive manner he would henceforward deploy for the fictional treatment of political issues—a wide-eyed, deceptively guileless wonder at the scenes he has invented and the brutality of which men are capable. Alternating between material essentially personal and material political and social, he adopted in succession a variety of authors as models, abandoning each in turn, until he found the tone that, in *One Hundred Years of Solitude,* would unify and transform personal memories and political convictions.

García Márquez's first stories are a disaster of Kafkaesque experimentation with physiologically rendered psychological states, but after an unrequited flirtation with Faulkner (*Leafstorm,* 1955), his social and political interests emerged, and with Hemingway, Camus, and his own journalistic experience as guides, he moved to a chastened, reduced surface in one good and one very fine novel (*In Evil Hour,* 1962; *No One Writes to the Colonel,* 1958) and a masterly collection of short stories (*Big Mama's Funeral,* 1962). In two of the stories of that collection ("Balthazar's Marvelous Afternoon" and "Montiel's Widow"), he abandoned his hard-won effaced narrator for a narrator arch and skeptical, adept at slight but telling exaggerations and ironic juxtapositions, who had already made his appearance in some of the journalism (most notably in the series "90 Days behind the Iron Curtain"). The journalistic ancestry of the new narrator is still more evident in the title story of that volume, "Big Mama's Funeral." In an elaborate parody of journalistic rhetoric through the observations of an ironic and disapproving commentator, García Márquez found a way to put to political use the penchant for events ostentatiously impossible and absurd that had been visible intermittently from the earliest fictions. Finally, in "The Sea of Lost Time" (1961), the translucent, skeptical, all-comprehending narrator of "Montiel's Widow" tells a simple tale of events both symbolically significant and impossible in the single work that most clearly augurs the narrative mode of *One Hundred Years of Solitude*. As García Márquez changed his narrative point of view, he also altered the way in which he managed the impossible or the marvelous, moving from impossible premises in the earliest stories ("The Third Resignation," "Eva Is inside Her Cat," "Night of the Curlews," "Someone Has Been Disarranging These Roses") through the naturalization of the impossible as dream or hallucination ("Eyes of a Blue Dog," "Nabo, the Black Man Who Made the Angels Wait," "One Day after Saturday," "Monologue of Isabel Watching It Rain in Macondo") to the marvelous real proper, the rhetorical heightening of events decidedly odd, but not impossible ("Balthazar's Marvelous Afternoon," "Montiel's Widow," and "One Day after Saturday" again). In the longer fictions prior to *One Hundred Years of Solitude,* he confined the marvelous or the odd to descriptions of characters or situations and to characters' speeches (the doctor's request for a dinner of donkey grass in *Leafstorm,* Pastor's feathery death in *In Evil Hour,* the office of the colonel's lawyer and the colonel's warning about the wearing out of roosters in *No One Writes to the Colonel*). There seems, then, to have been a disciplining of the author's disposition to the marvelous, as the marvelous ceases to express inner states, whether of the author or of his characters, and begins to symbolize external realities and to define realistic characters.

Dividing these early fictions into "personal" material and "sociopolitical" material had perhaps best be left to the author's promised memoirs, but in interviews and through Vargas Llosa, he has provided enough biographical infor-

17

mation to make it clear that by the late 1950s the personal had disappeared into the sociopolitical and that the two kinds of material, readily distinguished in the earlier fictions, had now become inextricable. The political transformation of the colonel-grandfather figure between *Leafstorm* and *No One Writes to the Colonel* is familiar and transparent enough, but a more interesting case appears in the maternal line in the treatment of García Márquez's grandmother in "Bitterness for Three Sleepwalkers" and of his mother and himself in "Tuesday Siesta." "Bitterness for Three Sleepwalkers" treats the ambivalent responses of the adult children of a family to the senile decay of their mother. Using an ill-defined "we" as narrator, García Márquez makes his family-narrator appear radically unsympathetic because the responses they articulate to the situation are so inadequate to it. "She," the mother, appears a prisoner, an object, until, in a sudden shift, "we" express a last, pathetic wish that a girl child be born in the house so that "we" could believe "she" had been born renewed. The biographical germ of this story seems to have been the decay of García Márquez's own grandmother in his parents' house, repeated in Ursula in *One Hundred Years of Solitude,* and the peculiar narrative technique seems to have been a means of coping with a certain ambiguity of feeling, expressing simultaneously the author's complicated dislike of such degeneration and his dislike of his own dislike. "Tuesday Siesta," on the other hand, is a brief and stringent celebration of the stoicism and courage of a woman of the people and her daughter in the face of economic deprivation and the violent death of an only son and brother, the support of the family. It requires no biographical information to make its events or tone comprehensible, and the only mystery that surrounds it is why, good as it is, García Márquez should say that this is his favorite among all his short stories. That preference may derive from the biographical origin of this story in the momentous trip the author made with his mother to Aracataca to sell his grandmother's house. He was not a girl, he was well over twelve years old, and no one had been shot breaking into a widow's house; but the return to Aracataca and the house in which he had been raised, so different in memory from its present reality, provided the story's central situation of unbearable isolation under a blazing sun and aroused in García Márquez the desire to write the story of the decayed house and town that would become *Leafstorm* and later *One Hundred Years of Solitude.* But crucial as this event was to García Márquez as man and as author, it has disappeared altogether into another story with its own clear and unambiguous political, social, and human purpose.

Of the earliest stories, Vargas Llosa has said that their problem is the lack of a story, and he attributes that lack to the very young artist's repudiation of his own immediate experience as subject, which forced him to fall back on his reading, in this case Kafka. These storyless stories also refuse, deliberately, to specify the usual components of stories: time, setting, character, names, relationships between characters. But no writer can evade his own experience altogether, not even a would-be Kafka, and García Márquez rejected his external biographical experience, whether as a child, adolescent, or young man, in favor of a symbolization of internal experience that comments on the quality instead of the events of that experience. To this preference of symbolic over self-regarding autobiographical representation, we owe the distinctive achievement of the later fictions, but in the earliest tales the symbolization turns inward, rendering an idiosyncratic, private condition rather than setting up a reverberation in our common experience.

Of the first three stories, two are complementary explorations of solitude and powerlessness, familiar themes in García Márquez's later work, pursued through situations that will become images in the later work. In "The Third Resignation" the protagonist is a young man who died seventeen years earlier at the age of eight and has continued to grow in his coffin. The cessation of growth marked a second death but brought with it the sudden fear that he would now be buried alive. The third resignation is the third death, the acceptance of his powerlessness to protest his remission to the earth. "Eva Is inside Her Cat" inverts the terms of the first: instead of life, the heroine rids herself of her beauty; instead of being fixed in a coffin, she is everywhere and nowhere, a point of consciousness; instead of a mere seventeen years of death, she lives 3,000 years of dispersal; instead of accepting a final death on the other side of fear, she is awakened to a consciousness of time's passing by the surge of an ungratifiable desire for the taste of an orange. Obviously, such characters do not act in the world in relation to other characters but exist only in the mind, and in the mind only as it is aware of an abstract state, death or beauty, fear or desire. To render the psychological state of his characters, the author depends almost entirely on the characters' awareness of physiological sensations, reducing the mind to a neurological center, aware of the smell of violets or formaldehyde, the contractions of the viscera, or a hot prickling like ants crawling under the skin. Situation substitutes for action, physiology for emotion, and bodies for character. It is not a happy substitution, particularly when we consider that although a young man may feel that his life is a living death, no young woman has ever wished to rid herself of her beauty—complained of it, repined at it, pitied herself for it, yes! but willed it away, never. Time takes care of that for her, she knows. But in spite or perhaps because of this lapse with respect to the truths of feminine psychology, these bodily situations correspond to a profound sense of solitude and powerlessness. Solitude defines the characters' circumstances in the young man's inability to communicate with his mother when she measures him and in Eva's escape into atemporality from her beauty, insomnia, ancestors, and the memory of the dead boy in the ground. Powerlessness reaches to the body itself. Before we discover his moribund immobility, the hero of "The Third Resignation" suffers a painful noise in his head that he would like to grasp, fling away, and cannot. Eva can neither reconcile herself to her beauty nor find her cat to eat her orange. Solitude and powerlessness will remain the dominant polarities of García Márquez's fictions even when he is exploring that most powerful of figures, the eternal dictator, and in the later fictions corpses will appear beautiful, undecayed, and heavy; men will fear burial alive; beautiful young women will be oblivious to their beauty and disappear into the atmosphere; physiological sensations will be poeticized as icy fungi or lilies growing in the gut; but the characteristic tone will have been transformed. While solitude will remain irremediable, while characters will always be trapped in the decaying body and entangled by nostalgia, the later characters will have something to lose, some relationship, activity, or memory to which they grapple. But these characters have no system of locomotion: they are possessed of a fear of dying without a motive for living.

The twenty-year-old author seems to have recognized the problem, for slowly, very slowly, his characters begin to move. In "The Other Side of Death" our hero lies in bed, awake, alive, though his twin brother is dead in the ground and that is what is on his mind. By "Dialogue with the Mirror," he has found a job and has gotten up to shave in front of a mirror that reflects his movements before he makes them, as breakfast cooks in another room. And although "He must have thought—since no other state of mind occupied him—about the thick preoccupation of death" and, of course, his dead brother under the ground, the morning sun on the garden is drawing him "toward another life, which was more ordinary, more earthly, and perhaps less true than his fearsome interior existence."[1] In "Bitterness for Three Sleepwalkers" the restricted narrative "he" has become a barely identifiable "we," but there at last materializes a character separate from the central consciousness of the story in the aged, senile mother. The invention of a character and the determination to turn to a more ordinary existence served him well, for in "Eyes of a Blue Dog" our customary young man returns, but in relation to another character—he has found a woman, though they meet only in dreams and she will not let him touch her, in spite of undressing in front of him and in spite of searching for him hopelessly when she is awake. "Eyes of a blue dog" is the phrase that would let them find each other outside the dream, but within the dream, she knows that she remembers it waking and he does not, for "You're the only man who doesn't remember anything of what he's dreamed after he wakes up" (154; 59). As that concluding sentence indicates, "Eyes of a Blue Dog" integrates dream and commonplace, catching what in real circumstances would be an unrealistic complaint and turning it into the reasonable complaint of a woman in unreasonable and well-defined circumstances. For, with one exception, from

1. *Innocent Eréndira and Other Stories*, trans. Gregory Rabassa (New York: Harper and Row, 1978), p. 131. *Todos los cuentos (1947–1972)* (Barcelona: Plaza & Janés, 1976), p. 45. Further citations from these editions will appear in the text, that to the English edition preceding that to the Spanish.

this story on García Márquez leaves behind the early vagueness that attempts to suggest great things by blurring outlines and solves the problem of plotlessness, as it must always be solved, by the invention of characters in conflict with one another.

The single exception is his first "political" story, "The Night of the Curlews" (1953), which reverts to the deliberate uncertainties of the stories prior to 1950 in an attempt, it seems, to intimate the powerlessness of the common people relative to the atrocities perpetrated by the powerful when their fellows will not believe what has happened to them, though it is reported in newspapers and visible on their bodies. Three nameless men, sitting in a courtyard, are blinded by curlews. No one will help them; no one believes their story, regarded as a newspaper trick to raise circulation. The child who identifies them as the men whose eyes were plucked out by curlews refuses to guide them home lest the other boys throw stones at him. Instead, he goes back to reading *Terry and the Pirates,* like the policeman in *In Evil Hour.* The men finally sit down in the sun, waiting for it to burn their faces before moving back to the wall. The curlews are explicated in *Leafstorm:* at the end of that novel, the boy remembers that Ada has told him that curlews sing when they smell a dead man, and the boy expects all the curlews to sing as the door is opened. One of the blinded men had been imitating the song of the curlews when they attacked. It is a claustrophobic little tale, the reader, like the characters, having lost "the notion of distance, time, direction" (182; 95), the central event never described, the world reduced to walls and gropings, the resolution deliberately irresolute. Instead of rendering a highly particularized world within which symbolically significant or allusive events take place, the author has, in his first excursion into symbolic politics, tried to imitate the sensation of helplessness from the inside, from the point of view of the victims. The perpetrators remain unnamed and insignificant. In the terms of the story, no crime has been committed; there is only a failure of solidarity on the part of the townspeople. That failure parallels the response of Macondo to the banana massacre in *One Hundred Years of Solitude,* though the novel is more sympathetic to the terrorized town than is this story. But the townspeople here, as in *Leafstorm* and "Tuesday Siesta," are rendered with considerable hostility as potentially or actively malevolent, suggesting a profound change in García Márquez's attitude toward "the people" as he and his fictions became more determinedly political.

When García Márquez's first ten stories were pirated in the early 1970s under the title *Eyes of a Blue Dog*, he advised his readers not to read them, but if they must, to steal them from the bookstores. Since then, he has authorized their republication in his collected stories and their translation. That change of heart was probably economic, but it would be pleasant to think that, like the fondness he expressed for *Leafstorm* after *One Hundred Years of Solitude*, he recognized in them his first attempts to play various narrative tricks he would master in *The Autumn of the Patriarch* and that he has forgiven them for being so jejune. Except for "Isabel Watching It Rain in Macondo" (which had been removed from *Leafstorm* and developed as a separate story), "Nabo" is the only one of the early stories to have been translated and republished with the author's permission before the appearance of *The Autumn of the Patriarch*, after the publication of *One Hundred Years of Solitude*. Earlier than "Isabel," it is also the only one of the early stories to exploit all the devices appearing in these stories that would reappear in *The Autumn of the Patriarch*. Like "The Other Side of Death," "Nabo" experiments with internal shifts in narrative point of view. Like "Bitterness for Three Sleepwalkers," it adopts a communal "we" for part of the narrative; ("Bitterness for Three Sleepwalkers" uses the communal "we" throughout). And it alone plays with the extended sentence containing shifts in point of view and juxtapositions of different times.

But since "The Other Side of Death" is earlier than "Nabo" and is distinctive in its experimentation with shifts in narrative point of view, let us begin there, more especially since it provides a glimpse, perhaps, of the origin and fate of the patriarch's double in *The Autumn of the Patriarch*. The story begins in the restricted third person, but as the nameless character begins to remember the dream from which he has just awakened, a textbook surrealistic dream, he begins to comment on it in the first person: "They were traveling in a train—I remember it now—through a countryside—I've had this dream frequently—like a still life, sown with false, artificial trees bearing fruit of razors, scissors, and other diverse items—I remember now that I have to get my hair cut—barbershop instruments. He'd had that dream a lot of times but it had never produced that scare in him" (107; 20). Later, as "he" begins to think about his dead twin in the ground, the resources of typography are called upon to effect an identification between the "him" narrating and the "him" in the ground as he recalls his brother's death throes: "Many hours had already passed since the moment in which *he saw* [narrator] him twisting like a badly wounded dog under the sheets, howling, biting out that last shout that filled his throat with salt, using his nails to try to break the pain that was climbing up *him* [brother], along his back, to the roots of the tumor. He couldn't forget *his* [brother] thrashing like a dying animal, rebellious at the truth that had stopped in front of *him* [ambiguous], that had clasped *his* [brother] body with tenacity, with imperturbable constancy, something definitive, like death itself" (110; 22–23). In *The Autumn of the Patriarch*, this dead twin will lose his own life in the patriarch's and will again die a terrible death in front of the survivor, but the narrative shifts will define character and relationships among characters and will impel the action onward. Here the shifts form part of a retreat from action: suddenly awakened, instead of getting up, our hero runs through his dream, remembers and identifies with his dying brother, and descends to the earth with him as he begins to wait for his own death. The movement outward, away, becomes a spiral that leads back into the self and ends in paralysis; but, while other people may wait for the patriarch to die, he himself will have none of it.

"Nabo" confines its shifts in point of view to an alternation between an omniscient narrator and a communal, familial "us" that first appears a third of the way through the story. As in "Bitterness for Three Sleepwalkers," the use of a communal voice serves to communicate hostility toward that voice by denying it affective responses in a story charged with pathos at other levels. The story turns on loss, on communication begun and broken between Nabo and the black man in the band who reappears as the hallucinated angel and, more importantly, between Nabo and the mute girl who learns to speak his name. But the communal voice has no share in that communication; "He was no longer delirious, but he kept on talking until they put a handkerchief in his mouth. . . . When we took out the handkerchief so that he could eat something, he turned toward the wall" (217, 79).[2] In the first part of the story, the pathos implicit in Nabo's predicament is relieved by the comic nagging of the angel that he hurry up and join the choir. But as Nabo's relationship with the mute girl is developed, the uncomprehending, uncaring "we" appear to correct the pathos, to control and check it, suggesting the author's resolute resistance to sentiment, as the other relationships in the story suggest his strong impulse toward it. Given that the family in "Nabo" has fed and housed a mad former servant, now useless, for fifteen years, a considerable degree of art has gone into making the reader remember only that they gagged him and tied him down.

"Nabo" might also seem to anticipate *The Autumn of the Patriarch* in its temporal shifts, but its use of those shifts is closer to *Leafstorm* than to the later novel in that the different times are juxtaposed rather than entwined. The same absence of fluidity marks, but does not mar, the experimentation with the extended sentence in the story's final, one-sentence paragraph (thirty-nine lines in Spanish, forty-six in English). The sentence relates a continuous movement, Nabo's bursting out of his room, but its progress is interrupted momentarily by the insertion with dashes (parentheses in the translation) of different times and the thoughts of different characters. In its last third, however, when Nabo has reached the backyard without finding the stable, the sentence shifts brilliantly and smoothly back to the girl in the room who cries out his name. Though the technique will be carried much further in *The Autumn of the Patriarch* and "The Last Voyage of the Ghost Ship," it serves in all three cases to reveal an exhibition of helpless power, to bind together endings and beginnings that contrast brutality and an epiphany, to evoke a moment, its history, and the response to that moment, all in a single syntactic unit, a headlong verbal act to contain a headlong physical act.

The line of progress in García Márquez's technical development is from the short stories to the novel *No One*

<hr>

2. The English version of "Nabo" appears in *Leafstorm and Other Stories*, trans. Gregory Rabassa (New York: Harper and Row, 1972), p. 217.

Writes to the Colonel, but, like scientists, artists do not proceed in a straight line to major discoveries. They make false starts, have to redefine what it is they are looking for, invent, and discard. *Leafstorm,* García Márquez's first novel, is one of those false starts: a technical dead end, important as the first attempt to deal with the materials of *One Hundred Years of Solitude* and, as is usually said on these occasions, instructive in its failures.

At the lexical level, García Márquez provides for the first time a town named Macondo, a banana company that brings enormous prosperity and leaves devastation in its wake, a slaughter of townspeople, a Señora Rebeca who is immured in her house, a Colonel Aureliano Buendía who commanded the Atlantic forces in the War of a Thousand Days, a windup toy ballerina, an Indian named Cataure and another named Meme, the Duke of Marlborough in tiger skins, a French doctor who eats grass like a donkey, a wife with manners more refined than those of the household into which she has married, biblical references to the deluge and the day of judgment, the promise of a final wind that will destroy the town, and the intimation that a prophecy is being fulfilled by the events of the narrative. This list does not exhaust the ties to *One Hundred Years of Solitude* and does not begin to enumerate those to the other fictions. Structurally, *Leafstorm* anticipates *The Autumn of the Patriarch* in the use of a brief temporal frame (one-half hour versus twenty-four hours in the later novel) that encloses all or much of the lives of the characters in the fiction; and the frames are parallel: the preparation of a body for burial, coupled with anticipation of the reaction of the townspeople, hostile in the earlier case, joyous in the later.

As the prologue to the novel makes clear, the author's purpose was to relate the history of the town as well as of the household, but the method he chose was the Faulknerian interior monologue, divided among three characters in eleven numbered sections with twenty-eight shifts of speaker, including one section at the beginning of III that seems to belong to "us," "we" who conclude the prologue and represent the founding families of the town, inundated by the "leafstorm." Other passages that seem to belong to that voice, at the beginning of VI and VII, are eventually and appropriately assigned to the grandfather, the colonel, as the head of one of the founding families of the town. The other speakers are a ten-year-old boy, who begins and ends the novel, and his mother, Isabel, abandoned by her husband, the daughter of the colonel and his first wife, who died giving birth to Isabel thirty years ago. The three are in the bedroom of the house in which the French doctor who ate grass like a donkey hanged himself the night before, as the colonel prepares to carry out his promise to bury the doctor in spite of the hatred of the town that wants to smell him rot aboveground. To fulfill his promise, the colonel has bribed the mayor to authorize the burial, denied at first from fear of the townspeople, and has summoned his four Guajiro Indian servants to coffin the body and carry the coffin. The novel ends after the door has been opened and as the Indians lift the coffin to their shoulders: the confrontation anticipated by those inside between them and those they imagine outside, the rest of the town, is now about to occur. We never see it, but only the tension of expectation in the color of the colonel's neck and the knot in the boy's stomach.

Within this frame, the author represents the ugliness of lives in a hierarchically ordered, static small town, devastated and demoralized by the disappearance of the leafstorm of the title, the inundation of wealth and people brought suddenly by the banana company that vanished as inexplicably as it came. The social structure reaches from the colonel and his family at the top to the vagabond woman who lived for two years in the hut behind the church at the bottom, by way of such representatives of the middle class as the barber and of authority as the priest and the mayor. The quality of life is epitomized in such events as the townspeople's rancorous mobbing of Meme when she goes to mass dressed as a lady, Isabel's being married by her father to a man who is still a stranger to her after a year's engagement, the malicious gossip that makes the doctor, because of his newly shined shoes, a suitor to the barber's mad daughter who believes herself impregnated by a spirit, the little boys' game of peeping in the windows at Lucrecia who, seeing them, sits on the floor and pulls up her nightgown until her mother chases the boys away, more impatient than angry. It is a stifling world of resentments, hostility, indifference, and isolation, the last embodied physically by the doctor's barricading himself in his house and verbally by the boy's private words that only his friend Abraham can understand and his wonder that his mother and grandfather "understand their words" (115; 100).[3]

The difficulties arise in the management of the interior monologues, and the source of the problem is that García Márquez wanted to use his speakers as historians as well as voices. Successful monologues depend altogether on tone, the communication of attitudes that define simultaneously the speaker and the situation. A corollary is that the monologuist must be highly verbal, his voice idiosyncratic, colorful, in some way distinctive. When Gárcia Márquez's model for the narrative structure and the syntax of the prologue, Faulkner, copes with inarticulate characters in such a novel as *As I Lay Dying* (Cash, Jewel), he surrounds them with others more articulate in an intricately graduated hierarchy of linguistic competence, some of it quite beyond the realm of the possible. In *Leafstorm*, the speakers have to carry so much exposition that distinctiveness of tone is lost in the byways of past events. Only Isabel exhibits a well-defined attitude toward the present situation: "I shouldn't have brought the child" (20; 13). The child is in the very awkward position of having to think about himself thinking and to observe himself as if he were standing beside himself observing himself: "And I stretch my legs out side by side and look at my own black and shiny boots. *One of my laces is untied,* I think and I look at Mama again. She looks at me too and leans over to tie my shoelace" (27; 19). The colonel is preeminently a man of reserves and silences, strong-willed, determined, singularly unsuited for the self-revelations of the form, though he makes an excellent effaced narrator in his own sections. The burden of exposition forces the characters out of distinctive voices, but they are also not characters who constitute their world in words. Essentially laconic, they live in a world in which a man can live with them in their house for five years before anyone realizes that no one knows even his name, and there is no evidence that, upon the realization, anyone asks. Indeed, the most successful technical aspect of the novel is the revelation of failures of communication at all levels, whether between characters or between characters and the reader. The stepmother will never tell

3. *La hojarasca* (Montevideo: Arca, 1965), p. 100.

her husband, the colonel, or the reader who she thought the doctor was; the colonel knows what the message the doctor carried said, but no one else does; the colonel, the doctor, and the reader know that Meme was pregnant by the doctor, but no one else in the family does; everyone in town knows what caused the slaughter of the townspeople, but the reader does not. But, as *In Evil Hour* and the later stories demonstrate, meaningful omission has nothing to do with the technique of the interior monologue and can be managed as effectively with other narrative techniques. When García Márquez returned to the extended monologue, he did it right, with the single bravura fling of Fernanda in *One Hundred Years of Solitude*. Comical, self-revelatory, a set piece as monotonous and miraculous as the rain to which it is a response, Fernanda's monologue seems to be an acknowledgment of Faulkner's earlier importance, an allusion of form, by an author who had left that influence behind, but who still thinks that *The Hamlet* is the great South American novel.

From Faulkner, García Márquez transferred his stylistic allegiance to Hemingway, the master of effaced narration who had learned much about leaving things unsaid from the prolix master of the unspoken, Henry James. The change of style was accompanied by a change of subject matter, a more deliberate and explicit treatment of the social and political questions that had formed part of the milieu of *Leafstorm*, but were not in themselves objects of attention. In "Two or Three Things about the Novel of *La Violencia*" and "A Man Has Died a Natural Death" (on the occasion of Hemingway's suicide), García Márquez specified the elements in Hemingway that had made the greatest impression on him: the objectivity of his style, the experiential base of his subjects, the image of a fiction as an iceberg, in which the tenth above the surface, all that is visible to the eye, suggests the far greater mass below. In his fictions, the influence of Hemingway manifested itself in the abandonment of first-person (singular or plural) and restricted third-person narration for an omniscient but largely effaced narrator; in increasingly economical, specific, and significant description; and in spare but clear plotting that produces the "iceberg" effect.

García Márquez had used an omniscient narrator in one story written before *Leafstorm*, "The Woman Who

Came at Six o'Clock," and was to do so again in one story written before *No One Writes to the Colonel*, "One Day after Saturday" (published as part of *Big Mama's Funeral*). But it is in *No One Writes to the Colonel*, most of the stories of *Big Mama's Funeral*, and *In Evil Hour* that García Márquez explores and exhausts, for his purposes, what Hemingway had to teach him. That this new direction was highly self-conscious is suggested by the change of setting in the fictions after *Leafstorm* and "One Day after Saturday." After those stories, only "Big Mama's Funeral" takes place in a town named Macondo. In *No One Writes to the Colonel*, the colonel left Macondo on "Wednesday, June 27, 1906, at 2:18 P.M."[4] Tied to the myths of a personal past, García Márquez seems to have felt that Macondo was not the place to explore the stylistic possibilities of impersonality. But the colonel left on the return train, and in "Big Mama's Funeral," the author returned to Macondo for a communal celebration, a funeral, that announced simultaneously the end of the life of privations depicted in the stories of the volume "forever and ever" and the end of rhetorical privation in the fictions of García Márquez.

But the abrupt stylistic transformation between *Leafstorm* and *No One Writes to the Colonel* was not exclusively an act of will. García Márquez had had six years of experience as a journalist between the two books, experience providing practice in the lessons of Hemingway, trained in the same school. Although it was not published until 1955, *Leafstorm*, according to Vargas Llosa, was written in 1951. *No One Writes to the Colonel* was completed in 1957, after García Márquez had laid aside a four-hundred-page version of *In Evil Hour*, begun in 1956. He returned to *In Evil Hour* in 1959, shortened it and purged it of "Faulknerisms," and in 1962 gave it its present title. It had earlier been called "This Shitty Town," a name that could be applied with equal justice to the town in which most of *Big Mama's Funeral* takes place and to the Macondo of *Leafstorm*.

The gain in clarity, efficiency, and effectiveness between *Leafstorm* and *No One Writes to the Colonel* is almost

---

4. *No One Writes to the Colonel and Other Stories*, trans. J. S. Bernstein (New York: Harper and Row, 1968), p. 59. *El coronel no tiene quien le escriba* (Mexico City: Era, 1961), p. 73.

miraculous and is immediately apparent in the novels' opening paragraphs. *Leafstorm* begins with a complicated temporal loop performed by a small boy, who begins with the announcement that he has seen a corpse, but immediately tracks back to the action of leaving the house:

> I've seen a corpse for the first time. It's Wednesday but I feel as if it were Sunday because I didn't go to school and they dressed me up in a green corduroy suit that's tight in some places. Holding Mama's hand, following my grandfather, who feels his way along with a cane with every step he takes so he won't bump into things (he doesn't see well in the dark and he limps), I went past the mirror in the living room and saw myself full length, dressed in green and with this white starched collar that pinches me on one side of the neck. I saw myself in the round mottled looking glass and I thought: *That's me, as if today was Sunday.* (15; 9)

We are given a great deal of information, but like the boy's repeated action of looking at himself in the mirror, the paragraph does not go anywhere, but instead winds back into itself in the manner of the earlier stories. The speaker is identified as a schoolboy; his physical and psychological experiences are linked (the varied discomforts provided by the suit and collar, the sight of a corpse, and his confusion about time); his family relationships and the order of precedence in the family are established. Grasping at specificity in the green corduroy, grandfather's cane, and Mama's hand, the paragraph provides a holistic experience, capturing the situation from a variety of angles, just as the boy thinks about seeing himself thinking about himself in the mirror. And we learn almost nothing about the character of the boy or the nature and significance of the experience he has just had.

The first paragraph of *No One Writes to the Colonel* reduces the objects in the picture, sharpens the focus, and initiates an action that continues forward:

> The colonel took the top off the coffee can and saw that there was only one little spoonful left. He removed the pot from the fire, poured half the water onto the earthen floor, and scraped the inside of the can with a knife until the last scrapings of the ground coffee, mixed with bits of rust, fell into the pot. (9; 7)

More economical, the paragraph also tells us more about

the character: his rank, his poverty (scraping the can down to the rust that intimates the age and husbanding of the can), the discrepancy between what he expects and what he finds (having to pour water out), and his habit of adjusting to that discrepancy (pouring the water out). Sentence structure has been simplified, and every syllable is relevant to the subsequent unfolding of the colonel's learning to resist as well as accommodate, though his resistance is only the continuation of his waiting by other means.

Set in the context of *la violencia,* the novel's seven sections chart the seemingly desultory progress of the colonel from October to December as he copes with the conflict between his desire to feed himself and his wife and his desire to keep for the January cockfights the rooster of his dead son, Agustín, shot down nine months earlier at a cockfight for distributing clandestine literature. The grim complexity of the political situation that prevails in the colonel's town is rendered laconically, often ironically, and exclusively through the speeches and actions of characters: the naively hopeful colonel; the skeptical, dissident doctor; the young, eager, and conspiratorial companions of the colonel's dead son; the venal Sabas and his half-mad wife; and the colonel's stalwart but despairing wife. All are defined by their language, from the colonel's wife's "We are the orphans of our son" to the doctor's "The only animal that feeds on human flesh is Sabas." The colonel himself has the best or at least the most comical lines, from his likening air travel to a carpet to his wish that Europeans and his countrymen could trade places so that each would be able to read about his own country in the newspapers. And the state of the colonel's bowels in October receives as much or more attention than the prevailing state of martial law.

The colonel is a quixotic figure and a most unlikely revolutionary, with his inexhaustible patience, his hair that stands up like a parrot's crest, his conviction that roosters wear out if you look at them too much, and his inimitable lawyer crawling on hands and knees under the pianola to find the colonel's power of attorney. But impelled by hunger and the importunity of his wife, he finally takes action on the pension he has been waiting for for fifteen years and tries to change lawyers. Like the government, the new lawyers do not write, and the colonel falls back on attempting to sell the last items of value in the house, a clock and a picture. That failing, he yields to the temptation of the wealthy Don Sabas, a member of the colonel's party who had made a deal with the authorities that enabled him to buy up the property of his fellow partisans forced out of town. Sabas names nine hundred pesos as the value of the rooster, but when the colonel finally bites, the offer has fallen to four hundred, which the colonel nevertheless accepts and from which he takes a sixty-peso installment. But before the rooster and the remaining money change hands and the deal is closed, Sabas goes out of town, and the friends of the colonel's son commandeer the rooster for the trials. At the trials, the rooster lives up to his reputation, and the intensity of the ovation, out of all proportion to that of the fight, seems at first farcical to the colonel. But in the pit, as he reclaims his rooster, and on the walk home, old, unspecified memories revive, and he decides to keep the rooster. There follow two days and nights of resistance to his wife's outrage at his decision, until she finally shakes him, demanding, "And meanwhile what do we eat?" for the cockfights are forty-four days away, and, as she suggests, the rooster may even lose. The novel concludes:

> It had taken the colonel seventy-five years—the seventy-five years of his life, minute by minute—to reach this moment. He felt pure, explicit, invincible at the moment when he replied:
> "Shit." (83; 121)

Shit is what the Colonel has been eating most of his life, but now he means to eat it, literally if necessary, and for a purpose.

It is a supreme act of will, this final, transforming determination to embrace sacrifice instead of merely suffering the sacrifices imposed by circumstances over which the colonel has no control. But it is also curiously ambiguous. A pyrrhic victory, it is a gesture toward self-annihilation for the sake of a symbol, another gesture. With the town channeling its resistance passively into the symbolic figure of the rooster, the spark of resistance may be kept alive by the colonel's determination, but a spark is only a spark, not a conflagration. Further, the colonel's decision has condemned his wife as well as himself to a diet in which she has not acquiesced. Innocent and childlike as the colonel may be, he has preferred the service of a symbol to a human obligation, and, win or lose, he has chosen not only the shit of deprivation but also the shit of glory consumed by, among others, the patriarch himself.

The sense that political heroism is problematic and that resistance is often futile though always necessary may account in part for the absence of a protagonist converted to political action in García Márquez's other novel of *la violencia, In Evil Hour.* Through discontinuous episodes featuring the town's leading citizens, he renders reactions to a plague of pasquins that put in writing and on doors the secret, common gossip of the town. The pasquins are not in themselves political, but, like the rooster, they symbolize resistance to the order imposed upon the town. The mayor is unable to stamp them out or to find the culprit (who is "the whole town"), and, as an image, the pasquins suggest that writing itself is subversive, especially the sort of writing that tells aloud what everybody already knows and does not say. Elegantly constructed, the novel opens and closes with the priest, who should know everything, being informed in his church of events that have escaped his knowledge, and the first response to the pasquins is a crime of passion. The mayor, the priest, and the judge, those pillars of the community, figure in most of the ten unnumbered sections, and each section introduces yet another leading family or citizen, catching them up one after another as the novel rolls from the passionate murderer whom the mayor forces to buy himself off to the sad, poor, and young Pepe Amador, caught distributing clandestine flyers, who is murdered in jail and buried in secret by the police. The novel's penultimate scene exposes the town's return to open warfare, declared by the mayor in his refusal to allow the doctor to perform an autopsy on Amador, whom the whole town, with no need of a pasquin, knows to be dead. In the first murder, the mayor had astonished the doctor by his observance of legal forms in summoning the doctor to perform an autopsy, but now those forms have been violated again, and with their violation has begun the disintegration of the order the mayor had hoped to restore. The novel ends with the jails full, the young men off to the mountains as guerrillas, and the implication that the town's doors are still littered with lampoons. Like *The Autumn of the Patriarch*, the novel treats resistance from the perspective of the powerless powerful, a method that reconfirms García Márquez's reluctance to celebrate triumphs he has not seen.

More importantly, however, the method illustrates the author's conviction that the horrors of *la violencia* were best portrayed indirectly, by suggestion and implication rather than by body counts and portraits of mutilations. Convinced that the novelists of *la violencia* had gone astray in their descriptions of men decapitated and castrated, women raped, genitals scattered and bowels ripped up (according to one eye-witness account, the purpose of genital mutilation was to prevent the procreation of more members of the opposing party), he argued that the story was not in the dead, but in the living "who sweat ice in their hiding places."[5] The insistence on indirection owes something to Hemingway's iceberg, as the choice of the central device of the pasquins does to the dictum that topics should originate in the writer's lived experience. (Pasquins had figured in the eighteenth-century uprising of Colombia's *comuneros* and more recently in Sucre, a town in the Department of Bolívar, one of the areas particularly hard hit, unlike the coastal provinces, by *la violencia*. García Márquez's family had lived in Sucre in the 1930s and 1940s.) But García Márquez also cited Camus's *The Plague* as a model of effective reticence, and formally the novel recalls Dos Passos's early radicalism in *Manhattan Transfer*, though with the scale reduced to García Márquez's and Faulkner's small towns.

The elaborate construction of *In Evil Hour* reappears in the order García Márquez imposed on the stories of *Big Mama's Funeral*, which describe a rising and falling rhetorical action of their own, complete with a surprising denouement, a perfect peripeteia in the final, title story. The rhetorical plot of the volume begins with three severely realistic stories concerning victims of increasing culpability, and as the responsibility of the victim increases, so does the author's irony, moving from the mother as a pure victim in "Tuesday Siesta" through the politically active dentist in "One of These Days" to the guilty Damaso in

5. Quoted in Mario Vargas Llosa, *García Márquez: Historia de un deicidio* (Barcelona: Barral, 1971), p. 134.

"There Are No Thieves in *This* Town." Then, in "Balthazar's Marvelous Afternoon," there suddenly appears a new tone in the stylized tale of Balthazar's exaggerated triumph and unexaggerated fall, a tone that moves to a still higher degree of stylization as the protagonist moves up the social and economic scale and becomes the widow of Balthazar's antagonist in "Montiel's Widow." In "One Day after Saturday" the stylization diminishes as we descend through the harmless and half-deranged upper classes, with Rebeca and the priest balanced against the boy who wants a pig farm, until in "Artificial Roses" we are back to the bleak and restrained mode in which the volume began. Then, altogether unexpectedly, there appears the final flourish of "Big Mama's Funeral" itself, and the lady's end signals the end of an era that is responsible for much of the suffering described in the stories that bear her name.

While the presiding genius of these stories is a monstrous woman, those in which the pain of existence is most unrelieved have as their central characters women whose only recourse in the face of their suffering is to bear it firmly and not to let others see how deep that suffering is. The mother in "Tuesday Siesta" with her peeling patent-leather handbag and "the conscientious serenity of someone accustomed to poverty" (88; 108), warns her daughter not to cry and resists, with quiet evidence, the priest's implication that her son, shot by the widow Rebeca as he tried to break into her house, had "gone wrong." She turns back that suggestion as imperturbably as she takes her daughter by the hand into the street where the townspeople have clustered to peer at them. Her counterpart is Mina in "Artificial Roses," whose young man has left her suddenly and without notice and presumably forever, and who resists with rancor her blind grandmother's attempt to penetrate and sympathize with her pain, throwing off invitations to intimacy as resolutely as she threw her lover's letters down the toilet. Like Ursula later, the blind grandmother sees without seeing and, knowing, sensing, everything Mina does, has surmised causes from effects. But in spite of her intrusiveness, she does not betray her granddaughter when Mina's mother enters, her arms full of thorned flowers that mock the artificial petals and stems Mina has thrust back into the sewing basket in this world where the roses are false, but the thorns are real.

The men seem to have more resources, though, by way of compensation, they suffer more physical pain. In "One of These Days" two pensive buzzards preside over the encounter between the mayor and the dentist who extracts, under duress, the mayor's abscessed wisdom tooth without anesthesia and "without rancor, with a bitter tenderness," saying "Now you'll pay for our twenty dead men" (101; 117). The mayor had been suffering that toothache since *No One Writes to the Colonel*, where he appeared briefly with his unshaven cheek, and, not content with the operation in *In Evil Hour*, García Márquez has had him have it out again. When the dentist asks whether to send the bill to him or the town, the mayor replies, in the story's last words, "It's the same damn thing" (102; 118), summing up the identity of power and venality that underlies all political action in these fictions, apotheosized in the patriarch's command to his wife's creditors to send the bills to the government. In "There Are No Thieves in *This* Town," that corruption takes an uglier form in the brutal beating of the Negro arrested for Damaso's billiard-ball theft and the bribe Gloria must pay to the mayor in order not to be arrested as an accomplice. She had unwisely told the mayor what all the girls in the house knew—that the Negro had spent the night with her and had not stirred out. Damaso himself, a pockmarked Valentino who lives off and occasionally beats his pregnant spouse, can find no better way to cope with the gap he has created in the town's amusements by stealing the billiard balls than to get caught in the act of returning them, but Roque, the poolhall owner who catches Damaso, promises another amusement. Roque had claimed that two hundred pesos had been stolen, "And now they're going to take them out of your hide, not so much for being a thief as for being a fool" (138; 145). The offences are very small, but the costs are very high, not only for Damaso, but also for Ana, his wife, and the girls who liked that pretty face and slender, agile body. In this town, romance does not flourish, and while our Macheath may not be hanged, he will be pulped.

The plotting of these stories is admirably efficient and resonant. Perfectly linear in construction, they begin with a

character in a situation, introduce a complication, and resolve it, while leaving unresolved and unchanged the essential dilemmas of the characters' existence: the mother's
poverty, Mina's loss, the dentist's hatred for the mayor
and what he represents, Damaso's desire for a new life and
some excitement. Vignettes of unimportant lives, they
speak of a singular plight to suggest that of a class, a world.
The only people who emerge with complacency and self-
satisfaction from these stories are the mayor and Roque,
the pool-hall owner, possessors of power and property.
The disequilibrium introduced into their lives by toothache
and theft, man and nature, has been happily removed.

"One Day after Saturday," though included in *Big
Mama's Funeral*, was written between *Leafstorm* and *No One
Writes to the Colonel*, and part of the problem it has presented commentators derives, I suspect, from disregarding
its date and treating it as contemporaneous with the other
stories in the volume. Sharing elements of the tone of
"Balthazar's Marvelous Afternoon" and "Montiel's
Widow," which it follows in *Big Mama's Funeral*, it is García Márquez's first attempt to resist the torpor of his invented town through the exploration of the marvelous
real. Its opening description of Rebeca's social position, its
analysis of the priest's failure to become a bishop, and its
quotation of Colonel Aureliano Buendía all manifest the
distinctive, evaluative narrative tone of García Márquez's
fictions from "Balthazar's Marvelous Afternoon" on to *One
Hundred Years of Solitude*. But the plotting is less mature.
The story articulates no resolvable conflict among its
characters and contains no significant political or social di-
mension against which to measure them. Instead, it uses
the marvelous to render character, principally the mind of
the dreamy priest (related to Big Mama by his family name
and ancestral to the first José Arcadio Buendía in his extravagant imagination) whose divagations issue in an absurd but compelling sermon on the Wandering Jew and in
an ineffectual act of charity, making over the church collection to the strange boy to enable him to buy a new hat.
The rain of dead birds, which sets things in motion, however unlikely it may seem, is so possible that it was repeated in San Francisco a few years ago and reported in the
New York Times, but its only functions in the plot are to
provide a means to contrast the characters of Rebeca and

the priest and to suggest that this is the sort of town in which birds die in the streets, in masses. That would be quite enough were it not for the irresolution of the conclusion, which, using the priest as a third-person reflector, imitates his confusion and does not adequately define the effect he has had on his parishioners. Rebeca believes him, others have said he has gone crazy, and they have all gathered, but what do they think? In "Tuesday Siesta" or *Leafstorm* what the town thinks or will do does not matter because the subject is the protagonist's determined disregard of the town. The town may be actively hostile or merely curious; it may act or it may watch: the protagonist does not care, and while the reader may care, he can rest without certainty, as the protagonist acts without certainty. But here the resolution turns on a new relationship established between the protagonist and the townspeople, and that new relationship is left betwixt and between. Though the half-mad upper classes may believe in his pestilential presence, García Márquez is not yet willing to convert his whole town to a belief in the Wandering Jew. The town will have to acquire a political consciousness in *No One Writes to the Colonel* and *In Evil Hour* before it will be allowed to reach that primordial simplicity.

By "Balthazar's Marvelous Afternoon" and "Montiel's Widow," the town has almost arrived. There is as yet no belief in the Wandering Jew, who will be trapped and burned in a later fiction, but there is a new simplicity and naiveté in the town's political attitudes. No longer a simmering pot of resistance to be treated solemnly and respectfully, the town and its people have become a stew of simple class resentments, grudging at and submitting to the rich most of the time and looting them when the opportunity offers after the death of Chepe Montiel or, as Balthazar's Ursula advises, setting extravagant prices on their birdcages. What accounts for this transformation is in large part, I suspect, the demonstration by the Cuban revolution that socialist revolutions are possible without the conversion of the people to Marxist-Leninist principles or even to the regular and surreptitious reading of clandestine literature. If revolutionaries can be relied upon to make revolutions where there is some but certainly not a universal politicization of the population, the writer need not duplicate their efforts. He need neither represent the people as an imminently revolutionary force nor persuade them to become an imminently revolutionary force by representing them as if they already were. That release from the weight of moral obligation carries with it no necessary literary consequence; it cannot explain the specific direction García Márquez's writing has taken. But it may account in part for the alacrity with which he turned to representations of the people as politically unsophisticated, and the persistence with which he has adhered to such representations, focusing his political imaginings not on the people as a force for change, but on the powerful as fools, hucksters, or monsters who must be annihilated and who will be, at least in the fictions.

The defining characteristics of García Márquez's later style that appear in "One Day after Saturday," the evaluative narrator, the marvelous real, the laconic quotation, also appear in the reportage contemporaneous with that story, particularly in the pieces on La Sierpe and El Chocó in 1954, isolated regions, cut off from the rest of the country by intractable terrain. In El Chocó, the Pacific province of Colombia where it rains 360 days a year and the maps diligently plot fantastic, imaginary roads that begin from nowhere and arrive nowhere, García Márquez was staggered by the useless fertility and mineral wealth of a region so isolated, met a man who announced that he was the national mail, and found the *chocoanos* obsessed by a single, overwhelming desire—a road to break the circle of the jungle, whether it went to Medellín or Japan. In La Sierpe on the Atlantic coast, renowned for its wizards, he encountered in the legend of "The Little Marchioness" the model for Big Mama herself, a fabulously wealthy virgin whose cattle took nine days to pass by. Without stirring from her house, she could command a serpent to lie in wait for an enemy or raise the dying from their death beds, if she were given the precise location of the sick man. Although she could not raise those already dead, their souls not being in her power, she could live as long as she wanted, and as long as she wanted was a little more than 200 years. At her death, accompanied by fearsome celestial signs and bad dreams for her neighbors, she passed on to her preferred attendants most of her secrets except that of eternal life, and set her cattle spinning until they created an enormous swamp in which her treasures lie hidden. In addition to legends like those of the Marchioness and La Pacha Pérez, a professional mourner whom the devil turned into a serpent when she was 185 years old, the author met a man certain to become just such a legend after his death in Pánfilo, a professional reciter of the rosary at funerals whose recitations blended Catholic beliefs and local superstitions. Such discoveries in the author's adulthood reconfirmed the living existence of the marvelous reality he has claimed for his childhood, and, in the reportage, he makes no attempt to naturalize or explain away the wonders he has found but accepts them as part of the structure of life and belief in the region in which they flourish.

In "Balthazar's Marvelous Afternoon" and "Montiel's Widow," there are no folkloric impossibilities, but there are the beginnings of hyperbole and a new simplicity in the rendering of the town as well as the protagonist. Simple protagonists had appeared before in Father Antonio Isabel and the colonel to whom no one wrote, but in these stories for the first time the protagonist is immediately set in the context of a town that is equally simple, whether in its wonder in "Balthazar's Marvelous Afternoon" or its skepticism in "Montiel's Widow." In "Montiel's Widow" the long-suffering town is unable to believe that Chepe Montiel has actually died; he has to be walled up in the family mausoleum "for the whole town to become convinced that he wasn't playing dead" (150; 155). In "Balthazar's Marvelous Afternoon" the townspeople are anonymous gawkers, speaking with one voice or gathering in a benign silence: "The cage was finished. Balthazar hung it under the eave, from force of habit, and when he finished lunch everyone was already saying that it was the most beautiful cage in the world. So many people came to see it that a crowd formed in front of the house, and Balthazar had to take it down and close the shop (139; 147). In their newfound naiveté, the townsfolk are also more sympathetic than they have often been in other stories, and they remain so in spite of the purely economic origin and the inconsistency of their political attitudes. What makes Balthazar's afternoon marvelous is the celebration in the pool hall with the men who believe he has gotten sixty pesos from Montiel. Like the colonel's rooster and with a similar epiphany for the hero, Balthazar's presumed coup is a symbolic triumph for them all, but the author seems now more skeptical of its efficacy: "Everybody toasted Balthazar's health, good luck, and fortune, and the death of the rich, but at mealtime they left him alone in the pool hall" (149; 154). Toasting simultaneously Balthazar's fortune and the death of the rich suggests a somewhat primitive and altogether natural analysis of the distribution of wealth and the desirability of its redistribution. And in "Montiel's Widow" it is precisely such an analysis that goes into action after Montiel's death as the widow's heifers disappear: "Bandits again" (156; 159).

But while the town's political attitudes may have become simpler, the narrator's relation to his material has become more complex. Simultaneously ironic and sympathetic, the narrator of these stories is less interested in the realistic representation of character or a social context than in the symbolic significance of characters' actions, and his principal vehicle for that significance is hyperbole. "Everyone" agrees that Balthazar's birdcage is the "most beautiful" birdcage "in the world," and García Márquez's ubiquitous, skeptical doctor calls it "a flight of the imagination." "No one" can believe that Chepe Montiel is dead, and "everyone" except his widow wishes he had been shot in the back instead of expiring in a rage like that which Balthazar had induced a few pages earlier.

Where the stories differ most sharply is in the kind and quantity of symbolic freight they carry, and García Márquez's greater experience in a realistic mode enabled him to manage his closure more successfully in the story less fraught with political cargo. Both fictions counterpoise two or more "readings" of reality, Balthazar and the town's against José Montiel's, the widow Montiel's against the town's and her husband's. But Balthazar's flight of the imagination brings him most emphatically down to earth. Although he has had his moment, he is worse off at the end of the story by a watch, a pair of shoes, the money in his pockets, and two weeks' labor. By returning him to a realistic context, the conclusion that levels Balthazar avoids sentimentalizing his victory or claiming too much for the power of the imagination. In "Montiel's Widow," however, the ending is almost as enigmatic as that in "Eva Is inside Her Cat," for it leaps to a suggestive, aggressively symbolic conclusion that would work if it could be connected with anything earlier in the fiction, but since it cannot be connected, dòes not. In the widow Montiel's lucid view of the inadequacy of creation, owing to God's unconscionable resting on the seventh day when there was still work for him to do, and in her outrage at the mayor's brutality, absolving her deeply implicated husband, she and her inventor illuminate both the dynamics of oppression and the miraculous though not uncommon ability to remain unaware of oppression while attributing violence only to its political source, forgetful of its economic roots. Perhaps because she has never in her life been "in direct contact with reality" (152; 156), the widow Montiel has an impeccable heart. But García Márquez has a problem putting an end to her in the last few paragraphs. The widow Montiel has been nodding agreement with her daughters's letters that one can't live in a country where people kill each other for political reasons. There follows a paragraph on the butcher shops of Paris and a sentence in a hand not her daughter's, "Imagine! They put the biggest and prettiest carnation in the pig's ass" (158; 160). For some reason, that amuses the widow Montiel. She then takes her rosary, falls asleep, dreams of Big Mama, asks her when she will die, and is told, "When the tiredness begins in your arm" (158; 161). The purpose is obvious: to close the story by making it open out, to end the story of the oneiric life of the widow Montiel in a dream, to promise the wearing out of the strong arm of power. Much can be said about that ending, but it is a deliberate non sequitur that shifts gears without putting the bridle on: it moves abruptly from one kind of symbolic context to another kind, instead of resolving in the same mode. In all probability, García Márquez was consciously avoiding having Big Mama say anything too obviously circular and referential, but would that she had.

In "Big Mama's" own "Funeral," García Márquez solves the problem of closure by a prior determination to sweep her off the earth forever and ever. But he accomplishes this momentous task at the expense of the transparency of his narrative voice. "Big Mama's Funeral" is rhetorically the richest of the fictions, with sentences as overstuffed with carnival details as if they were sausages. The biggest and prettiest carnation goes in the pig's ass. For the first time, he adopts the technique of summing up a lengthy action before it occurs, which he will use again only in parallel contexts, when he is about to decimate such political operators as Colonel Aureliano Buendía and Senator Onésimo Sánchez. And he discovers a number of images that will reappear in the history of Big Mama's male equivalent, *The Autumn of the Patriarch*, including the ending, from the grandees' wrangling through the buzzards and the dismantling of the house to the birth of a new era. The folkloric impossibilities of La Sierpe have been politicized, and the wizards of La Sierpe and the banana workers of Aracataca form part of the national procession arriving at Macondo. Even the frame device of *One Hundred Years of Solitude* appears for the first time: the story told. But the narrative voice is a peculiar one, unique to this story, and its failure to be fully satisfactory may account for García Márquez's initial decision to have the patriarch do the talking in *The Autumn of the Patriarch*. Leaning against the doorway, telling the story before the historians get to it, the narrator establishes a disapproving distance as well as an ironic one between himself and his material, as if it were necessary to articulate clearly, without any possible ambiguity, the voice of opposition to Big Mama and what she represents. When that hortatory voice is out of the way, as it is most of the time, the rhetorical elaboration of allusive absurdities carries the attitude perfectly well all by itself. There is no danger that anyone will miss the significance of the items in Big Mama's visible and invisible estates, power's perquisites and Colombian commonplaces, or of the appearance of Colonel Aureliano Buendía's veterans, overcoming their centenarian hatred of Big Mama to ask the President of the Republic for the pensions they have been waiting for for sixty years. Since the story represents a pageant, however, rather than an action, García Márquez has developed within it no opposition, communal or individual, to Big Mama with which his narrative voice can sympathize. As a result, the narrator obtrudes, identified only with his own aperçus and essentially isolated. In both *One Hundred Years of Solitude* and *The Autumn of the Patriarch*, the author will situate the narrator partly within the fiction and will not leave him sitting in the doorway, blocking the reader's way in.

While "Big Mama's Funeral," like *Leafstorm*, contains an astonishing number of details that will reappear in *One Hundred Years of Solitude*, including the first glimpse of an incestuous tangle, it is in "The Sea of Lost Time" that García Márquez pulled together impossible events, political purpose, and the transparent narrator. While "Balthazar's Marvelous Afternoon" and "Montiel's Widow" exploit hyperbole for a political purpose through the same narrator, none of their events is impossible, nor are any of the episodes within the action symbolic, though the structure of the action as a whole may be. In "The Sea of Lost Time," however, García Márquez has retold the story of the leafstorm in an entirely symbolic mode and in three parts, two perfectly clear and the last perfectly obscure. The two-thirds that are perfectly clear take up the transformation of a desolate town by imperialism in the form of foreign investment that looks as though it is giving money away and ends by fleecing the nation, in other words, by taking out of the country in profits sums far in excess of the original investment. Tobías, kept awake by crabs, smells one night from the useless sea a scent of roses that is gone in the morning. Like the boy in "The Last Voyage of the Ghost Ship," he puts himself to watching the sea, waiting for it to come back, as it eventually does. Soon that miraculous smell lures Mr. Herbert, the philanthropist, and masses of others to the town, but as Mr. Herbert falls asleep, the odor disappears, and the town empties out again. While Mr. Herbert was awake and active, he gave money away, according to his promise, in return for the recipients' doing whatever it was they did best. From imitating birdcalls, the performances become rapidly less innocuous, as in Mr. Herbert's finding a hundred men at five pesos each for a grandmotherless, nameless Eréndira who needs five hundred pesos and who, with Tobías's help, wrings out a mattress that will be wrung out again in *One Hundred Years of Solitude* and again in Eréndira's story. Continuing to give money away, Mr. Herbert ends by owning all the property in town. The interpretive difficulties begin when Mr. Herbert wakes up and takes Tobías on a turtle-fishing expedition to the bottom of the sea that gives the story its title. Millions of turtles rest on the bottom, alive but sleeping for millions of years; a happy town on a Sunday afternoon is filled with roses; the beautiful dead wife of old Jacob floats past; and Tobías sees, as fish do, the whole sea upside down, reflected as in a mirror when he looks up to the surface. Given the title, we seem to be in the realm of transforming memory, always there and always below the surface, the sea where the dead are, but also the sea of the happy town. There remain forever the happy town of childhood, undone by a cataclysm, and the old woman, restored to youth, and as beautiful as García Márquez's grandmother is said to have been. What Mr. Herbert would be doing in that sea, however, is far from obvious, and he is evidently in his element, swimming easily, like an octopus, and warning Tobías not to tell about what he has seen, because if people knew about these things, there would be great disorder above. From the reader's point of view, the sea appears to represent one thing to Tobías and another to Mr. Herbert, master of its resources, who brings up an enormous turtle, slaughtered with great detail and difficulty, to feed them all. Symbols, perhaps, are like that, and the story seems to be an attempt to integrate the personal and the political through symbolic and impossible episodes.

García Márquez himself appears to have been dissatisfied with the attempt, since he wrote no more stories for four years and did not authorize the republication of this story until 1972 (nor, perhaps more significantly, its translation until 1974; it might have been included in the *Leafstorm* volume, but was not). What seems to have balked him was a double problem with closure and the integration of materials. Not suprisingly, it is the political action that is most lucidly and efficiently rendered. For memory and the place of the past, however, there are not yet equivalent actions; there are only images. Fine things, but not sustaining, they float past memorably enough, but since they have neither beginning nor middle, it is difficult to supply them with an ending. The story concludes in the tentative, modernist manner of the earlier realistic fictions, as Tobías tells his wife of the town at the bottom of the sea. She not only fails to believe him, but also silences him, telling him not to start up with his wild imaginings again. So, Tobías, rejected, lies awake at the edge of the bed until dawn, bothered by crabs, just as he was at the beginning. Such an ending is appropriate to the political action, but inadequate to the trip to the bottom of the sea, which demands a finality congruent with its artifice. García Márquez's problem seems to have been finding a formal pattern adequate to contain magical and symbolic events, and he solved that problem with a novel that is all pattern.

For the revolutions in García Márquez's style that end in *One Hundred Years of Solitude*, there is an allegory to be read in the figure of Colonel Aureliano Buendía, who began as an avatar of Rafael Uribe Uribe, the liberal general under whom the author's grandfather had served in the War of a Thousand Days. Always a figure of prestige, regarded with awe by the characters in the fictions, he was named but did not appear in *Leafstorm, No One Writes to the Colonel*, "One Day after Saturday," "Tuesday Siesta," and "Big Mama's Funeral." But we all remember how *One Hundred Years of Solitude* begins: "Many years later, as he faced the firing squad, Colonel Aureliano Buendía was to remember that distant afternoon when his father took him to discover ice." That mythical, lofty figure has been removed from the idealized periphery of the fictions and placed squarely in the center to be shot at; and although he escapes the firing squad, his myth is badly tattered in the course of the novel. Entering and controlling the consciousness of a figure who had dominated the imaginations of his own earlier characters, García Márquez has subdued to his own fictive purposes both the private mythology of the Márquez family and the extrinsic, public demand for political heroes in fiction, even to denying his family's and his own hero the heroic death promised by his opening words.

III. AT HOME IN POPE'S GROTTO: *ONE HUNDRED YEARS OF SOLITUDE*

> Let us roll all our strength and all
> Our sweetness up into one ball,
> And tear our pleasures with rough strife
> Thorough the iron gates of life;
> Thus, though we cannot make our sun
> Stand still, yet we will make him run.
>   Marvell, "To His Coy Mistress"

After such an epigraph, the reader may expect a sententious discourse on total novels, biblical and apocalyptic structures, the meaning of life, love, and time, or at the very least the self-betrayals of a self-destroying narrator. All in good time: before we embark in such heavy weather, we should know what made the crew sign on for the voyage. For it has been some time since a novel simultaneously made the best-seller lists and precipitated a critical industry. Naive or sophisticated, the reader who enters *One Hundred Years of Solitude* encounters a world he has not been allowed since childhood, provided he was lucky enough to have had a childhood rich in fairy tales. The novel begins, it is true, with a man in perilous circumstances, before a firing squad, but by the end of the first sentence we have gotten to his childhood, and in a few sentences more we are back to our own: a world in which we do not yet know the names of things, and so we must point; a world in which magnets are wonders that put to shame the magnets that in most schools are still one of the first encounters that children have with the mysteries of science; and finally the world of fairy tale proper, in which a wise and beneficent magician or fairy godmother, Puck, cat, or caterpillar takes on the initiation of the young and a couple reverse the roles of the fisherman and his wife as the husband sets out on the endless quest for gold that motivated Jack, Dick Whittington, the lady who did not want to marry Rumpelstiltskin, and Pizarro.

Although the novel returns us to childhood's sense of discovery and infinite possibility in a world determinedly unlike the realistic worlds of the novels of our adulthood, it is not childlike, if that term suggests an attempt to re-create some putative lost innocence and freshness, as in a few of

Wordsworth's ballads or Blake's *Songs of Innocence*. Instead, García Márquez captures us by recapturing for us the "'satiable curiosity" of childhood, a curiosity that is inseparable from the child's or the adult's desire to increase his power by increasing his knowledge, and increase of knowledge is the subject of the novel's first chapter, as José Arcadio Buendía leapfrogs his way with Melquíades's aid through the major stations of the progress of science in the west, from the Greek magnets and magnifying glasses to the Portuguese navigational equipment that long ago discovered the new world in which the seeker lives, with Melquíades's last surprise a parodic discovery of the long-sought fountain of youth in a set of false teeth. Paradoxically, of course, and it is one of the things that makes this a novel for grown-ups, José Arcadio Buendía increases his knowledge as, in direct consequence, his power in the world diminishes.

Also for grown-ups, the novel contains lots of sex and violence, coupled with that indispensable attribute of the best-seller, rapidity of movement. But if this were all, while we might have a best-seller, we ought not to have a critical industry. What the sophisticated reader, and critics at their best belong in that category, has always demanded of literature is that it delight and instruct, be at once natural and new, and, in our own twentieth century, reconstitute our vision not only of the world but also of literature. And García Márquez seems to have managed it. At the very least, he has written a book that integrates most of the theoretical concerns of modern literature and criticism and that could be taken as a textbook illustration of the fruits of modernism, a work that clearly descends from the multifarious and contradictory impulses that inaugurated twentieth-century fiction and that is also very clearly something quite different from any of its progenitors. Unlike his great antecedents, however, García Márquez has not, or so it seems to me, opened up new possibilities for other writers; rather, he seems to have closed off certain avenues, though he may of course have imitators. Certain aspects of his rhetoric are, like Milton's, dangerously imitable, and the end he has accomplished, the representation of a bizarre, complex, and complete world, tempting.

If we take García Márquez's own earlier works as representative, derivative, late modernist pieces and contrast them with *One Hundred Years of Solitude,* we see that of the many differences, the most striking are the unity and the clarity of the later work in the management of similar characters, themes, and concerns, whether in the use of a mythically allusive structure (to *Antigone* in *Leafstorm*) or in the emphasis on history, memory, isolation, dream. In the earlier works, those concerns find a fragmented form in accordance with the author's models and the mimetic assumption that since modern life is chaotic, disorderly, and obscure, our fictions should be so too. *One Hundred Years of Solitude* moves us further into the twentieth century by inventing an internally coherent system, the constitutive members of which mean nothing outside that system or apart from it, while the coherence of the system itself (supported by its references to what we know of our world) satisfies our desire for meaning. The enterprise of the novel thus parallels the work in other fields of Foucault, Lévi-Strauss, and Barthes in that nothing is ever explained (how does historical change occur? why does this tribe prohibit these foods?), but everything makes sense by being put in new patterns of relationship. And our pleasure in those new patterns depends on our seeing rearranged in them things we know or thought we knew.

To achieve that unity and compose his system, García Márquez made use of more than two structural principles, but let us begin with the most general and the most specific, a pair that conveniently marries the Hellenic and the Hebraic. The novel traces the history of a family, the Buendías, and a town, Macondo, from their origins sometime in the nineteenth century to their obliteration sometime in the twentieth, with allusions to a prior history of the founding family extending to the late sixteenth century. Over this family, a fatal curse looms, harrying them down the generations: the threat of the birth of a child with a pig's tail as the result of violating the incest taboo. Atreus and Oedipus presiding, this is the plot device on which the novel turns, and the fulfillment of the curse ends the action of the novel. This Hellenic concreteness is contained, however, within a Hebraic abstraction, for the book as a whole is modeled on the biblical movement from Genesis and Eden to Apocalypse by way of history and prophecy. Our first glimpse of Macondo is pre-Adamic and Arcadian, things lack names in a primitive, egalitarian idyll before "original sin." Mixing Cain and Moses, the founders come to a land no one had promised them because one of them has killed a man, and the murderer stops in Macondo because he has dreamed of a great city. (Cain is the founder of cities.) Thereafter, we descend into history in the violent complications of nineteenth- and twentieth-century politics, with events prophesied before they occur, plagues, a deluge, and a final "apocalyptic wind," a "biblical hurricane" that ends the novel by destroying the town and the last Buendía, who is really a Babilonia and thus related to the scarlet whore with her cup of abominations, who is a great city, fallen.

Within the larger biblical structure, there are several kinds of historical structures: the history of Western science from magnets to airplanes, the history of Latin America, the history of Colombia, the history of literature. José Arcadio Buendía's progress is miraculous until he reaches his own time and time stumbles and stops for him, as it did, metaphorically, for the continent after independence. But, from outside, arrive electric lights, the cinema, gramophones, telephones, automobiles, though the airplane is sent to the homophonic Makonde (which seems a little unfair, since Colombia did have the first airline in both the Americas). Discovering Macondo, the founders repeat the discovery of America by the Spanish, as they become "the first mortals" ever to see the western slope of the mountains, and the tie is confirmed by the discovery of the skeleton in armor and the galleon beached inland. Though the armor is fifteenth century, the first record of Buendías and Iguaráns is in the late sixteenth century, the century in which Colombia was explored and its cities founded. Colonel Aureliano Buendía takes us through the nineteenth-century civil wars with references to *la violencia* in his plans for agrarian reform and his desire to join with Victorio Medina; Aureliano Segundo and José Arcadio Segundo lead us through the leafstorm and the Ciénaga massacre in the twentieth century. The history of Western social organization is recapitulated in the patriarch and Renaissance man, José Arcadio Buendía; the heroic military leader, Colonel Aureliano Buendía; the bourgeois family man with his well-kept mistress, Aureliano Segundo; the radical labor organizer, his twin, José Arcadio Segundo; the bookish, reclusive adolescent intellectual, Aureliano

Babilonia, so familiar from so much modern fiction. In literary terms, the same characters describe a trajectory from myth to epic to the novel, and each parodies the type that corresponds to his genre: the patriarch becomes useless when he becomes a Renaissance man; the Renaissance man destroys the pianola and misuses the daguerreotype to try to photograph God playing the pianola; the hero loses all of his wars; the bourgeois family man is kept by his mistress; the labor-organizer's career ends in a massacre and the disappearance of company and workers; the intellectual reads a manuscript that destroys him. There is also literary criticism: is the purpose of literature to show us new ways to prepare chick-peas, or is it the best plaything ever invented to make fun of people?

If we regard the novel for a moment as a grid, these are its horizontal lines, running the length of it, constituting its temporal structure. There are also vertical lines, composed of parallel characters, events, phrases, constituting its spatial structure. Very few things happen only once in Macondo. If it is predicted by an irritated Rebeca in her courtship with Pietro Crespi that Ursula will be buried in her rocking chair, Pilar Ternera is. If there is a historical massacre of banana workers, there is also a carnival massacre of nine clowns, four Columbines, seventeen playing-card kings, one devil, three minstrels, two peers of France, and three Japanese empresses. If a priest levitates with cups of chocolate, a beautiful woman rises into the heavens holding on to the family sheets. If "Her name was Pilar Ternera," then "Her name was Petra Cotes," and she too was the mistress of a pair of brothers, one of whom was more taken with her than the other. If the tenth chapter echoes the opening of the first chapter in a book with twenty chapters ("Years later on his deathbed Aureliano Segundo would remember the rainy afternoon in June when he went into the bedroom to meet his first son"),[1] then the twelfth chapter echoes the amazement of the inhabitants of Macondo at a new round of inventions, electric lights and movies. Uniqueness seems to belong only to the way in which characters die, and death itself is univer-

1. *One Hundred Years of Solitude*, trans. Gregory Rabassa (New York: Harper and Row, 1970), p. 174. *Cien años de soledad* (Buenos Aires: Editorial Sudamericana, 1969), p. 159.

sal. García Márquez insists on the recognition of this patterning through the confusion created at first by the repetition of masculine given names and by the alternation of personal characteristics belonging to those named "José Arcadio" and those named "Aureliano." But it should be pointed out that a masculine name is in fact repeated in identical form only once. The patriarch is always called José Arcadio Buendía; his sons are José Arcadio and Aureliano, later Colonel Aureliano Buendía; José Arcadio's son is just Arcadio; the only son of Colonel Aureliano Buendía who figures in the early part of the novel is Aureliano José, while his seventeen sons are identified by their mothers' last names, Aureliano Triste, Centeno, Amador. The only identical names are comically appropriate, suggesting an identity where there should be an antithesis: José Arcadio the macho, son of José Arcadio Buendía and Ursula Iguarán, and José Arcadio the homosexual, son of Aureliano Segundo and Fernanda del Carpio.

The women in the novel are for the most part more stable and sensible and at least as resolute and enduring as the extravagant, whimsical men to whom they are connected and whom they tend to outlive when there are no complications in childbirth (as there are with Remedios and Amaranta Ursula). Their names cause no confusion, and there is less emphasis on the recurrence of psychological traits, though there is such recurrence. Down the generations, however, the women are grouped in asexual-sexual pairs, opposed with respect to their psychological relation to sexuality or in their sexual action. Ursula opposes Pilar Ternera (though Ursula might also be said to have been raped by her husband, as Pilar was by the man who then kept promising to marry her); Amaranta opposes Rebeca; Remedios the Beauty, Remedios the child-wife of Colonel Aureliano Buendía; Fernanda, Petra. The opposition breaks down in more modern times, as both Meme and her sister Amaranta Ursula violate social convention, but Meme ends condemned to celibacy in a convent, punished for her sexual transgression by her mother. Amaranta Ursula is punished only by nature. Missing is Santa Sofía de la Piedad, who possesses the rare ability to exist only at certain moments, and who would seem not to fit, a common-law widow with three children, who smelled of her own flower lotion instead of Pilar's smoke when she sought out Arcadio in the dark as a replacement for Pilar, his mother, if she did not parallel Carmelita Montiel, a virgin bathed in orange water, who discovered that her cards were blank as she waited for Aureliano José, shot to death, whose aunt Amaranta she was to have replaced in his affections and with whom she was to have had seven children.

There are also, of course, parallels across the generations between Ursula as the builder of an aristocratic house that excludes the family of Pilar Ternera and Fernanda as an aristocrat who excludes anyone associated with the banana company; between Pilar and Petra, Rebeca and Pilar, Amaranta Ursula and Amaranta and Ursula and Rebeca: it can be set down as a rule that for any structural opposition of characters that the reader finds, there is another opposition that puts one of the characters in opposition with yet another character on the basis of a different set of attributes. Why does Gaston appear in Macondo with a dog collar around his neck, led on a leash by his wife? At this level of explication, because Gaston is to Amaranta Ursula and Aureliano Babilonia as Pietro Crespi was to Rebeca and José Arcadio: both outsiders, both technically skilled, one brings a new kind of business enterprise to Macondo, where love makes him settle, and the other plans to, and both are routed by a member of the family. Gaston's dog collar is Crespi's polite, assiduous passivity. Of course, there are also parallels between Gaston and José Arcadio as accomplished lovers who leave Macondo, and Pietro Crespi and Aureliano as pining lovers who stay. Nor should we forget that Fernanda's attempt to exclude the banana company and the failure of that attempt parallel José Arcadio Buendía's attempt to throw Moscote, the future father-in-law, out of town. Everything is mirrored by something, and as we read rapidly along, hurtling from one episode to another, we are jolted, sometimes lightly, sometimes powerfully, by the recognition that what we now see has happened before, what we now learn, we also remember. And when we reread the book, it fills not with recollections, but with anticipations.

When we ask what these repetitions mean, however, we run into a problem, for very often the echo adds nothing to our understanding of the immediate circumstances of the characters or the situation. When we respond to the pathos of Carmelita Montiel's loss, we do so fully without remembering Santa Sofía de la Piedad, though we may remember another scene that affected us in the same way, the death of Arcadio, dying a hero's death that we had believed reserved for Colonel Aureliano Buendía. But Carmelita Montiel's loss is individual; it belongs to her and is felt by the reader as a minor and utterly devastating cataclysm. Other repetitions do, however, have an immediate, local effect: on a second reading, when we are able to anticipate its historic parallel, the carnival massacre acquires a new horror. When the second half of the book begins with the people of Macondo dazzled once again by new inventions, we experience a little desolation that so much has happened and so little has changed, that we have lived through so many lives only to be taken back where we began, so little further on. And there may also be a bit of the horror we feel for Scheherazade when she begins to tell the same story over again: repetition is death. Sometimes repetitions make events more possible: Remedios the Beauty could not have risen into the heavens so easily, sheets or no sheets, without the assistance of the levitating priest. (In *The Autumn of the Patriarch*, Manuela Sánchez disappears without such assistance, or, in other words, precedent, and readers are sometimes troubled by it. But they are immediately reconciled to it when reminded of Remedios.) But the possibility of explicating repetitions in context, even if all of them could be explicated, as they cannot, does not explain why García Márquez has "constructed" a book rather than written one. By all our conventions of reading and analysis, patterns and repetitions are supposed to be hidden, subliminal, to be dug out by sharp-clawed critics and flourished to classes and colleagues. They are not to be plotted by the author so as to reduce the spoils on which our honor depends to the coprophiliac delight of digesting the novel to produce our own version of the drawerful of "working-notes, diagrams, sketches, and memoranda" that García Márquez unceremoniously consigned to a Barcelona dustheap "so that the way that the book was constructed shouldn't be known."[2]

2. Rita Guibert, *Seven Voices* (New York: Alfred A. Knopf, 1973), p. 326.

The marvelous events within the fiction present us with the same kind of difficulty: some of them can be explicated in place by a variety of interpretive maneuvers or by reference to García Márquez's earlier work; some, like José Arcadio Segundo's invisibility, seem permanently elusive. But the question is why they are there at all. Disappearing Armenians and flying carpets have obvious literary antecedents; a young girl with an exclusive diet of earth and plaster, to which she returns when anxious as an adult, can be readily explained in psychological terms, as can the insistence of incestuous desire. The trail of blood that winds from José Arcadio's ear to his mother Ursula in the kitchen has been explained by García Márquez as the umbilical cord (and its route corresponds to the way José Arcadio returned to his mother after his trips around the world), but I prefer to be reminded of a religious film that circulated in the 1950s and told the sad and terrifying story of a man who stole a consecrated wafer and desecrated it, only to find following him as he went about his daily business a trail of blood that led directly back to the bleeding wafer. After all, Ursula was making bread, blood finds her, and her son was sacrificed, all very sacramental, but I won't insist on it. García Márquez has said that the insomnia plague is political, referring to the ability of governments to control information and to liquidate the memory of their own transgressions; there are keys to memorizing objects and feelings written in all the houses, "But the system demanded so much vigilance and moral strength that many succumbed to the spell of an imaginary reality, one invented by themselves, which was less practical but more comforting" (53; 48). As the annihilation of all memory, it is a more sweeping case of what happens in the banana massacre, obliterated from the memories of the people of Macondo and from the schoolbooks of the regime. Melquíades the magician then reappears to restore memory to Macondo, as García Márquez the writer restores the memory of the banana massacre to us all. More generally, however, the insomnia plague is the loss of language, the loss of memories personal as well as political, the loss of history, of literature, of human reality itself: "They went on living in a reality that was slipping away, momentarily captured by words, but which would escape irremediably when they forgot the values of the written letters." Insomnia has plagued García Márquez's characters since "Eva Is inside Her Cat," but this is insomnia with a difference. The loss it threatens is not that little annihilation, the second death, sleep, but a total obliteration of everything from which García Márquez has made the novel: words, and through words, personal biography, national history and Western culture, books read, his own earlier works sacked for names, ideas, and events. Writing "solemn nonsense" on the walls (55; 49) is not enough to save Macondo and its memory; that requires the reappearance of a magician who is also a writer.

Both magical events and insistent patterning violate our expectation that fictions will be verisimilar and disrupt our easy submersion in an alternate world. When things happen in Macondo that do not happen in other places (or books), the reader is forced to ask, what does *that* mean? and should be reminded that he is reading. When we want to know what a work as a whole "means," we ordinarily abstract a pattern from its events, characters, and images in order to arrive at a generalization that we call the work's "meaning" and that serves to make a variety of elements that at first seemed unrelated cohere. We have "made sense" of the book. But when we try to abstract a pattern from *One Hundred Years of Solitude,* we find pattern itself, a pattern of repeated patterns. With so much in the fiction pointing to the fictiveness of the fiction, should the revelation at the end of the novel that the book is, indeed, a book, astonish us? Perhaps it should not, but it does; inevitable, it is also unforeseen. Besides, only two of the characters know about it, the author and the reader. The rest lived and died thinking they were alive.

At the end of the novel, then, a book that seemed to be holding the mirror up to nature (though some very odd things appeared in that mirror) turns out to be holding the mirror to itself. In the last three pages, the last Buendía reads the manuscripts of Melquíades, written during the course of the novel. The manuscripts of Melquíades tell the same story that the novel of García Márquez does, and as the reader of the novel of García Márquez finishes his reading, the reader within the novel finishes his. The separate times merge, the separate books become one.

One Hundred Years of Solitude, as we have seen, is a book that takes its shape from another book, the only book of which the name means book, and which was often called "the book" until it lapsed in the course of time into "the good book," as a result of competition with other books, though it remains a best-seller. Etymologically, *biblia* takes us back to *biblos, bublos,* "papyrus," the material on which *biblia* were written, and ultimately to *Bublos,* the Phoenician town from which the material was exported from Egypt to Greece. Within the book *One Hundred Years of Solitude,* there is a set of manuscripts written on parchment, and the author refers to those manuscripts by both the word for manuscript, *manuscrito,* and the word for parchments, *pergaminos.* It is the *pergaminos,* not the *manuscritos,* that Aureliano Babilonia reads at the end of the novel. Both *parchment* and *pergamino* originate in *Pergamon, Pergamum,* the town where parchment was first used as a substitute for *bublos, biblos,* "papyrus." By which we see plainly that the parchments of Melquíades are not the Bible.

What they are is the experiential center, in Helen Vendler's phrase, of the novel, telling the same story with the same disregard of man's conventional time, making separate events coexist in a single instant from the first sentences on, though the first sentences may be different: the only line Aureliano Babilonia reads aloud to us is the epigraph. (Printed, *One Hundred Years of Solitude* has no epigraph; but in manuscript, who knows?) Melquíades wrote the manuscripts after he came back from the dead to save the memory of Macondo. When he finished them, he proclaimed that he had found immortality and, shortly thereafter, drowned. José Arcadio Buendía, misunderstanding the significance of Melquíades's final instructions to burn mercury in his room for three days (mercury being a preservative of wit), was nevertheless certain that "He is immortal, and he himself revealed the formula of his resurrection" (76; 69). But Melquíades's immortality is that of literature, not the body. The body rots, and his is the first grave in Macondo. For the next hundred pages, throughout the wars, the manuscripts sit locked in Melquíades's room until, at the pleadings of the twelve-year-old Aureliano Segundo, the room is opened and revealed intact, untouched by spiders and dirt, luminous. After reading what appears to be the *One Thousand and One Nights,* Aureliano Segundo turns to the indecipherable manuscripts, and Melquíades reappears, instantly recognized by virtue of the memory inherited from, of course, his grandfather. But when Aureliano Segundo asks him to translate the manuscripts, Melquíades refuses, and the English reader is undone by a serious misprint. The English sentence reads: "No one must know their meaning until *he has* reached one hundred years *of age*" (177). But the Spanish sentence is: "Nadie debe conocer su sentido mientras no *hayan* cumplido *cien anos*" (161, emphases added). Preserving the structure of the English sentence, the translation should read: "No one must know their meaning until *they have* reached one hundred years of age," for the Spanish is altogether unambiguous; it is not the reader of the manuscripts who must reach one hundred years, but the manuscripts themselves. (If the English were accurate, we should have to congratulate Aureliano Babilonia on remarkable agility in his lovemaking for his age.) Thus, the title of the book refers not to one hundred years in the history of the family or the town, but to the one hundred years of the manuscripts, solitary as long as they are unread, solitary in the writing, solitary in the reading, unless read aloud. The Spanish sentence also contains a pun that the translation necessarily obscures: "No one must know their meaning when they haven't finished [reading] *One Hundred Years* [*of Solitude*]." Only when the reader finishes reading *One Hundred Years of Solitude* does he know what the manuscripts mean.

The phrase *one hundred years* appears only two other times in the novel, both referring to the manuscripts at the end, and one in another pun: "everything written on [the parchments] was unrepeatable since time immemorial and forever more, because races condemned to one hundred years of solitude did not have a second opportunity on earth" (383; 351). At first, the sentence is puzzling and a little contradictory: what races do have a second chance on earth? what is so special about people condemned to "one hundred years of solitude"? Only that they are condemned to existence in a book called "one hundred years of solitude" and have no existence outside it. Meanwhile, while we've been reading Melquíades's book, a fellow named Gabriel Márquez, who left Macondo and his girlfriend Mercedes some time ago for Paris, was last seen in his friend Aureliano Babilonia's imagination "writing by night to confuse hunger in the room that smelled of boiled cauliflower where Rocamadour was to die" (374; 342). What was Gabriel Márquez writing, and how does Aureliano manage to predict the death of Rocamadour in Cortázar's *Hopscotch*?

The written word is central to the book, and García Márquez has made that tautology the device on which the book turns and the justification of the proliferation of events that exist only in the imagination. When Melquíades returns from the dead to save the town from the insomnia plague, he has "lost all of his supernatural faculties because of his faithfulness to life" (55; 49). But a writer who is "faithful to life" does not allow his characters to come back from the dead. The writer who resurrects his characters has supernatural faculties. But when Melquíades's supernatural faculties are gone, he writes. Only the book has supernatural faculties.

But while the system may be internally coherent, is it any more than a neat trick? Is the novel no more than a highly ingenious, elaborately worked out *summa* of the author's earliest memories, furthest imaginings, and a theft from Thibaudet? As a novel, is it not a mere parody? The parody of genre has been mentioned, but the biblical structure is also parodic: there is no salvation at the end of this book. The sacred text does not restore to life, but destroys. The family curse, the violation of the primordial taboo, ponderous matters these, lead to what? The birth of a child with the tail of a pig, an event merely embarrassing, not impossible, not grievous, and not necessarily even fatal: the first time it happened, the child lived happily until the age of forty-two when, virginal, he had it cut off and bled to death, a simple case of death before the dishonor of a man's remaining forever a virgin. The compulsiveness and dangerous excitement of incest, emblematic of familial and personal solitude, does it mean anything more than the commonplace that Latins are particularly fond of their mothers,[3] that we all look for someone like ourselves as sexual object, or that incest is something we do not do

3. If this seems to the reader an unwarranted, racist stereotype, let me assure him that it is a warranted cultural stereotype and refer him to the songs about holding one's mother in one's arms in one's dreams by the Latin equivalents of James Taylor and Barry Manilow.

when someone else is watching? And is there not something peculiar about a book that represents solitude not as a psychological state but as a physical condition and reminds us of it on every page?

It seems a little hard to demand of a dazzling literary artifact that treats its own gravities with such irreverence that it be more than an artifact, particularly when it fulfills so many critical wishes. *One Hundred Years of Solitude* has, after all, given us a self-consuming artifact, liberated us from conventional time, insisted on the artificiality of the work, constructed an alternate universe governed by its own supernatural laws, deployed the word to destroy the word as well as the world, given dreams as much reality as telephones ringing in empty rooms, made impossible events *vraisemblable* by expressing them in grammatical sentences, prevented us from being able to name the speaker, suggested the arbitrariness of the relation between word and thing in the disjunction between patterning and what is patterned, and, to end on the American continent, mingled every mythos. In the novel, if we seek, we shall find "*Agon* or a sequence of marvellous adventures [as] the basis or archetypal theme of romance; *pathos* or catastrophe, the archetypal theme of tragedy; *sparagmos,* or the sense that heroism and effective action are absent, the archetypal theme of irony and satire; and *anagnorisis,* or recognition of a new born society, the archetypal theme of comedy."[4] In sum, a novel has been provided that fits—too readily perhaps—the tools of any critic. For those of the derrière-garde, there are irony and paradox, illusion and reality, character and point of view. For the left, there are criticism of modern history, political corruption, and imperialism, contrasted with the primitive equality of early Macondo, and the revaluation of incest that rejects the primordial use of women as property to be exchanged between families. For the right, there are the revolutionary turned despot, the intimation that the liberal rebels have fought for twenty years against the will of the nation, and the clear correlation between prosperity and the imperialist banana company, poverty and its absence. For the nihilist, there are the futility of war, the destruction of humanity in

4. Northrop Frye, *The Anatomy of Criticism* (Princeton: Princeton University Press, 1957), p. 192.

political action, and an ultimate resolution in total destruction as nature overwhelms men and art, indifferently. For the psychoanalytic, there are traumatic childhood experiences and the pervasive passion for aunts. For the Lawrentian, there is salvation in sex through love or love through sex. Surely, anything that has so much for so many must be nothing in itself. Cleopatra's variety may have been infinite, but her reputation has suffered for it.

Let us take the worst case, and leave aside the liberty García Márquez re-creates for our imaginations, the active movement of mind to which his events impel us, the scope and skepticism of his political and social concern, the aesthetic satisfactions of his structure. That subtraction leaves us with his characters (and their fates) and the demand that novels tell us about life as they show us art and before they tell us about it. And it might be objected at once that García Márquez's characters do very little to increase our understanding of human nature or the human condition, largely because of his refusal to explore character in the analytic modes to which we are accustomed or to represent characters who are, we fancy, like ourselves in self-conscious complexity. What has he to offer modern, urban man in this modern, urban age except a flight from the real to play? One response might well be to sniff that there are in this world far more people unlike us than like us and that the narcissism implicit in the objection merits a corrective. But that would be merely to insult, not to persuade, and it evades the charge of irresponsible evasion.

It would be pleasant to be able to say that García Márquez's rejection of the analytic exploration of character and his adoption of "objective," epic narration represent a conscious political choice against bourgeois and post-industrial–capitalist self-interest, but there is no evidence for it. As we have seen, the fictions prior to *One Hundred Years of Solitude* move from an unsuccessful, introspective mode to a highly successful, symbolic mode that is also comic. The successful short stories that are not comic use the same techniques for character representation as those that are: speech, actions, fleeting thoughts, brief comments by the narrator on the conclusions characters reach or do not reach, in other words, evidence and conclusions, with the process of reaching conclusions either omitted or abbreviated, never minutely, delicately, sensitively spun out.

The method is admirably suited for comedy, since it leaves a space for incongruity between speech and actions, motives and appearances. The sharper the discrepancy, the greater the comedy will be. To quarrel with this mode of characterization is to quarrel with the comic mode itself, as many people do in otherwise unaccountable preferences for Richardson over Fielding, Eliot over Dickens, Bellow over Pynchon. Like all comic artists, García Márquez works from a simple set of implicit positive precepts: in his case, the desirability of social, familial, and sexual love, honest government founded by consent rather than by force, the equitable distribution of wealth and property, a church that provides support for these positive values rather than working against them or allowing them to be undermined through its own inertia. (The conclusion of "Big Mama's Funeral" suggests the belief that the improvement of material conditions will create a world in which the church is not necessary, in the Pope's ascent to heaven, his mission fulfilled upon Big Mama's death, but the author does not insist upon it, for it has not appeared since.) Like all comic artists, García Márquez does not go about providing lists of his positive values; they emerge from their persistent violation in the fictions and in an occasional peroration about what has been wrong all these years and what will now be, and be right. Like the wedding or the dance in other comedies, that announcement rings the curtain down. But that is not how *One Hundred Years of Solitude* ends, nor are its characters the fixed types, the inflexible attitudes that constitute so many comic characters, great and small.

In *One Hundred Years of Solitude*, the comical is always shifting its location, from a character to a situation to an event and back again. Characters are sequentially absurd, noble, pathetic, vicious: it is Ursula, of all possible characters, who mangles the upbringing of Arcadio and the last José Arcadio. The novel renders human character in its ultimate opacity, human actions in their final incomprehensibility. The only mystery that is never solved in Macondo, the narrator tells us, is the death of José Arcadio, who shot himself or was shot by his wife or—though it is not mentioned as a possibility—was shot by some unknown, unpostulated third person. We have a mystery because we do not know what action occurred, but we also have a mystery because we do not know why either action should have occurred. It is a mystery of motivation. Such characters as Amaranta and Colonel Aureliano Buendía, Fernanda, and Aureliano Segundo reveal an enormous, twisted capacity for destruction and self-destruction, coupled with the ability to keep on living and acting in the teeth of their demolitions in order to die an inevitable, natural death in the bosom of the family. When Amaranta thrusts her hand in the fire or Colonel Aureliano Buendía suddenly remembers that he has ordered Moncada shot inside the barracks or Fernanda puts on her ermine cape, we understand the action and the character who performs it, but we also know that a thorough explanation of the act or the character would require a lengthy exegesis for which the novel provides much evidence and little or no argument. Nor are such acts comical, though two of them may be regarded as bleakly absurd, and each character is often comic. Like the characters in *Big Mama's Funeral* or the colonel and his wife to whom no one wrote, they are as much themselves as representatives of possible modes of behavior, the material of comedy. Reinforcing the complexity of the principal characters is the source of evil in the novel. Most of the vallainous acts are performed by members of the family with whom there is always sympathy. With the exception of Cortes Vargas and his anonymous army of "sons of the same mother" (280; 257) (more bitter, the translation reads "of the same bitch"), the stage villains are minor and comical—the black-frock-coated lawyers fluttering about Colonel Aureliano Buendía; the elusive, never-present Mr. Jack Brown. Instead of a panorama of different kinds of minor villains, the novel puts its worst acts in the hearts of its principals, in the cauterization of feeling in Amaranta and Colonel Aureliano Buendía, in the repressive, religious single-mindedness of Fernanda and the weakness of Aureliano Segundo who lets her have her will with their daughter Meme. This evil lurking in the hearts of men is ordinarily the stuff of tragedy or melodrama; when it appears in comedy, it is usually glossed as frailty or assigned to minor characters. But García Márquez has combined the singularity definitive of tragic experience with the cyclicity characteristic of comic experience.

The repetitive, cyclic pattern of the novel encloses

characters, lives, that happen only once. However many parallels there may be, nothing happens in the same way twice. The extermination of the seventeen Aurelianos, for example, seems designed to illustrate identity: each is killed when the cross of ashes on his forehead is penetrated by some lethal instrument, but in the five cases provided, four immediately, the fifth years later, the method of murder is carefully discriminated: Aureliano Triste is done in by a rifle shot in the darkness, Centeno by an icepick, Serrador by a revolver shot that knocks him into a cauldron of boiling lard, Arcaya by a Mauser, Amador with two shots from two Mausers fired by two policemen who have tracked him for years, and each was engaged in a different activity when he was slain. There is as much attention to difference as to similarity, and were we to count, we would find that there are more differences than similarities, as there are more sentences than sentence patterns. However much characters may have in common, however parallel their experiences may be, each passes through an unhappy, arduous history peculiar to him or her alone. From time to time, the onward rush of time is stopped momentarily when a character has an impression of recurrence, that this event has happened before, that time is going in a circle, but such moments are intermittent, not constant. Nor do they mean that time is going in a circle, but that it seems that time is going in a circle, for time, which may seem generously to loop back upon itself, never gives the individual creature a second opportunity. And so, in spite of the fans of the eternal return, in *One Hundred Years of Solitude,* time is linear, the town passes through chronological historical phases that reduce it to the nothingness from which it began, everyone dies (or disappears), and the book ends.

But there is of course more to it than that, for while characters recognize repetitions only occasionally, the reader sees them whenever he looks and sometimes when he doesn't, momentary sparks that seem to illuminate while the significance of the whole escapes. The temptation of such epiphanies is to make them mean something in themselves, but García Márquez rejects that impulse to transcendence and prevents the reader from yielding to it: the frequency of repetitions in his mirrored room prevents any single instance from gathering most of the meanings to itself and dominating the others.[5] The cumulative effect of such repetitions is to suggest that the irreversible, onward movement in which each character is trapped and which seems intensely individual to him and to us is nevertheless a common condition and that the perception of pattern, like the making of meaning, depends upon being able to step outside the flux and for a moment to stop it. But if repetition suggests the communality within the most varied experiences, it also denies the efficacy of any particular experience. When Aureliano Babilonia comes to her with his heart breaking for Amaranta Ursula, Pilar Ternera laughs. His suffering, tragic and unique to him, is comical to her because she has seen it before, as many times as the reader has, for Pilar has been there from the beginning, before Macondo, and has read the lives of the characters in their experience as well as in her cards (for a "century," though not "one hundred years"). While Melquíades predicts, Pilar recognizes that "the history of the family was a machine with unavoidable repetitions, a turning wheel that would have gone on spilling into eternity were it not for the progressive and irremediable wearing of the axle" (364; 334). Pilar is able to see the repetitions because, though badly worn herself, she has not yet worn away altogether. What makes the axle wear is time and the inevitability of endings in time for individuals, species, the universe, books, a common fate that picks us off one by one.

García Márquez's grandmother, he tells us, invented fantasies so that he wouldn't be saddened by the truth of things. One truth of things in *One Hundred Years of Solitude* is that the past is past and ends come, unimpeded by the fantasy that distracts us from that simple truth. When Aureliano Babilonia perishes as his past and present meet, he repeats the attempts of other characters to destroy the past when they have become mired in the present: José Arcadio Buendía takes a crowbar to the alchemical laboratory of his

5. For readers still puzzled by mirrored rooms, cities of mirrors, and speaking mirrors, a field trip to the Albright-Knox Museum in Buffalo, N.Y., will provide a visual aid in Lucas Samaras's "Mirrored Room," a full-size room walled with mirrors, with mirror table and mirror chair and mirror ceiling. Standing in it for a few minutes should make at least one thing perfectly clear.

imagination; Colonel Aureliano Buendía destroys "all trace of his passage through the world" (167; 152); Aureliano Segundo breaks every breakable emblem of domesticity in the house, from flowerpots to vases and china to the earthen jar in the kitchen, when Fernanda's monologue catches up to him. Their attempts at annihilation were premature, I would submit, because the author wanted to reach his own present, our own time, and the time of contemporary fiction before, with a wave of the pen, a tap of the typewriter, he made the vision disappear. But because those attempts were premature, like Aureliano Segundo's and José Arcadio Segundo's attempts to decipher the manuscripts, Aureliano Babilonia's annihilation is singular, the parallels break down, and the novel ends only once. But in that ending, it makes a singular experience double itself before our reading eyes, making a witticism of its own inevitable termination.

Comedy, more than tragedy, originates in direct opposition to the way of the world. It stays within that world to reorder the disorder of things while the tragic hero blazes his own way, often creating the disorder that the comic hero has to tidy up as best he can. So it is a rare comedy that ends in apocalypse, though there is a precedent in Pope's *Dunciad*. As that precedent suggests, the decision to annihilate suggests dissatisfaction with the world that has been created, but is the author's dissatisfaction political, personal, or fictive? I would suggest that it is all three: that it records a world like our own fundamentally unsatisfactory in both personal and political terms, and that the author is not dissatisfied with the world he has made, insofar as he has made it (in other words, the dissatisfaction is fictive, feigned). It is, moreover, past, and the decision to destroy it makes its inevitable disappearance into an act of will, an assertion rather than a submission.

For the world of the book redeems the sadness of things with the play of fantasy. Drawing attention to the resources of the imagination that go "beyond the genius of nature and even beyond miracles and magic" (11; 9), the fiction reminds us of the eternal gulf between what reality supplies and what the imagination can conceive by intersecting the plotting that ends things, as all things end in this world, and the patterning that makes circles, leaping into the future, back to the past, free of time and the constraints of the body, as only the mind can. More than a mirror and more than a lamp, the novel is reminiscent of that curious creation, Pope's grotto. To go from his house to his garden, Pope had to use an underground passage, and that master of rhetorical mosaic made it an emblem of his verse: he conveyed three streams to trickle melodiously through it, adorned the walls with shells, fossils, irridescent minerals, pieces of mirrors in angular forms, and hung an alabaster lamp from a star in the center from which "a thousand pointed Rays glitter and are reflected over the Place." A visitor moralized the grotto thus:

> Mr. *Pope's* poetick Genius has introduced a kind of Machinery, which performs the same Part in the Grotto that supernal Powers and incorporeal Beings act in the heroick Species of Poetry: This is effected by disposing Plates of Looking glass in the obscure Parts of the Roof and Sides of the Cave, where a sufficient Force of Light is wanting to discover the Deception, while the other Parts, the Rills, Fountains, Flints, Pebbles, & c. being duly illuminated, are so reflected by the various posited Mirrors, as, without exposing the Cause, every Object is multiplied, and its Position represented in a surprizing Diversity. Cast your Eyes upward, and you half shudder to see Cataracts of Water precipitating over your Head, from impending Stones and Rocks, while salient Spouts rise in rapid Streams at your Feet: Around, you are equally surprized with flowing Rivulets and rolling Waters, that rush over airey Precipices, and break amongst Heaps of ideal Flints and Spar. Thus, by a fine Taste and happy Management of Nature, you are presented with an undistinguishable Mixture of Realities and Imagery.[6]

In both, we see what we know not to be there, and the imagination is flooded by both the objects seen and the marvel of their production, the awareness of the monumentality of the fiction being perpetrated upon us. What use is it? There is only one misguided soul in Macondo who wants to put the "useless invention" of the magnets to use, and he is told "It won't work for that." *One Hundred Years of Solitude* will neither teach us a new

6. Maynard Mack, *The Garden and the City* (Toronto: University of Toronto Press, 1969), pp. 46–47.

way to prepare chick-peas nor make a revolution that transforms the world. But it may remind us that it is the mind's capacity for imagining what does not exist and its dissatisfaction with what does that are finally the only means by which the world is ever transformed.

IV. INTERMEZZI: INNOCENT ERÉNDIRA AND HER FRIENDS

> "Tis manifest, what mighty Advantages Fiction has over Truth; and the Reason is just at our Elbow; because Imagination can build nobler Scenes, and produce more wonderful Revolutions than Fortune or Nature will be at Expence to furnish. . . . How fade and insipid do all Objects accost us that are not convey'd in the Vehicle of *Delusion?* How shrunk is every Thing, as it appears in the Glass of Nature? So, that if it were not for the Assistance of Artificial *Mediums*, false Lights, refracted Angles, Varnish, and Tinsel, there would be a mighty Level in the Felicity and Enjoyments of Mortal Men.
>
> Swift, *A Tale of a Tub*, sect. ix

When he finished *One Hundred Years of Solitude*, García Márquez knew what his next novel would be. In 1968 he was learning how to construct an electric chair for the use of a character in that novel. In 1969 he had read so many histories and anecdotes of despots that he had to forget them all in order to write his own story of the solitude of the dictator. Originally, the novel was to take the form of the dictator's monologue before a tribunal of the people at the end of a reign of three hundred years in which, among other excesses, the dictator had served up his roasted minister of defense on a silver platter, in uniform and decorations, to ambassadors and bishops assembled for a gala banquet. Obviously, García Márquez made some changes, but he also knew from the beginning that the style of the work had to be different from that of *One Hundred Years of Solitude* and that it would be a denser and more difficult style. At one point, he joked that it would be in the style of Robbe-Grillet so that no one could understand it and he could be sure that it was a good novel.

Between the novels, he published two volumes of early reportage, *When I Was Happy and Undocumented* (1974) and *The Story of a Castaway who was ten days adrift on a raft without food or drink, who was proclaimed a hero of the nation, kissed by beauty queens, enriched by publicity, and then abhorred by the government and forgotten forever* (1970), and a volume of seven short stories, *The Incredible and Sad Story of Innocent Eréndira and her Heartless Grandmother* (1972), that included, in addition to the title story (1972), the earlier "Sea of Lost

Time" (1962), "A Very Old Man with Enormous Wings" (1968), "The Handsomest Drowned Man in the World" (1968), "Death Constant beyond Love" (1970), "The Last Voyage of the Ghost Ship" (1968), and "Blacamán the Good, Vendor of Miracles" (1968). It was an elegant volume, and it makes quite clear that García Márquez was writing himself out of the style of *One Hundred Years of Solitude* and into that of *The Autumn of the Patriarch* in 1968, while the two later stories seem to be something of a vacation from the intricacies of the dictator. Though the stories are very different from one another, they possess a common motif that suggests the discomfort of a suddenly fashionable author or "escritor de moda," as he styled himself in the preface to *The Story of a Castaway*: all treat an often uncomfortable relationship to crowds and focus on public figures, some of whom would rather not be public figures, though others seek it. Except for "Death Constant beyond Love," they also share a determined resistance to interpretation. In most cases, the dynamics of the plotting suggest certain thematic possibilities, but, written in a wholly symbolic mode, the stories are devised to repel the impertinence of any interpretations imposed upon them through the intransigence of the irreducible, impenetrable events or images at the center. While a great deal may be said about these stories, they have been designed to escape the critic's web of exegesis.

The same is true of *One Hundred Years of Solitude*, of course; the sense we make of it is as much an artifact as the thing itself. But because it juxtaposes its incomprehensible premises (why incest?) with comprehensible lives, we read past the impenetrable episode to which we cannot assign meaning, content with those to which we can, trusting that someday, like the theory of relativity, it will make sense and we will be able to understand it as well as talk about it, quote it, and use it for analogies. The difficulty is more obvious in the shorter forms, which, being shorter, do not provide as many escape hatches from the absurd impossibility of the invention at their center: an old man with wings, a ghost ship that materializes, a beautiful drowned man, an immortal huckster, a heartless grandmother with green blood. In "A Very Old Man with Enormous Wings" and "The Last Voyage of the Ghost Ship," an impossible event is made real; in "Innocent Eréndira" and "Death

Constant beyond Love," a possible event is made strange; and "The Handsomest Drowned Man in the World" and "Blacamán the Good, Vendor of Miracles" work both sides of the street. All of them deal with exploitation, credulity, and the force of illusion along the Atlantic litoral in the dry, dusty towns of the Guajira peninsula or in a city that combines the chained bay and slave port of Cartagena with the rotating light of Santa Marta. There are cross-references among the stories, images and characters that go back to *One Hundred Years of Solitude* and beyond it into the earliest fictions, devices the magpie author uses to suggest the integration of his fragmented world and to enhance the reflective power of the rhetorical surface by creating recognitions for the reader within the universe of the text.

In "A Very Old Man with Enormous Wings" and "The Handsomest Drowned Man in the World," both subtitled "A Tale for Children," García Márquez wrote out the stylistic vein of *One Hundred Years of Solitude;* in "Blacamán the Good, Vendor of Miracles" and "The Last Voyage of the Ghost Ship," he tried on parts of the style of *The Autumn of the Patriarch.* "Death Constant beyond Love" and "Innocent Eréndira," while more similar to the stories in the style of *One Hundred Years of Solitude* than to those in the later style, seem to be moving in yet another direction and may augur the mode of the novel García Márquez has written and thus far refused to publish while Gen. Augusto Pinochet is still in power, *Chronicle of an Expected Death.*

The most conspicuous of the stylistic innovations is in the management of the sentence and the paragraph. "The Last Voyage of the Ghost Ship" is a single sentence; "Blacamán the Good, Vendor of Miracles" is divided into seven paragraphs, but one-third of its sentences run over ten lines of text, and interminable as the paragraphs of *One Hundred Years of Solitude* often seem, there are more of them per page of text than in "Blacamán," while sentences that run over ten lines of text are rare. The principal exception is Fernanda's monologue, a two-and-a-half-page sentence. The page–paragraph ratio in "A Very Old Man with Enormous Wings" and "The Handsomest Drowned Man in the World" is the same as in the novel, while "Death Constant beyond Love" and "Innocent Eréndira" go back to the shorter, more frequent paragraphs of the fictions prior to

One Hundred Years of Solitude by the simple expedient of reintroducing and marking dialogue.

As the precedent in Fernanda's monologue indicates, one purpose of the inordinate sentence is to imitate the sound of a single voice. The method looks introspective, but is not. It is rhetorical, a representation of how the character consciously sees himself and represents himself to others. The character's self-presentation may betray him, as Fernanda's and Blacamán's do, but such betrayal follows from the character's ignorance of the implications of what he says or seems to think. The excessive sentence has other uses: to recall what someone else said in the past, imitating that voice; to represent an imagined interaction; to represent an interaction and dialogue taking place in the present. Only the first of these is present in Fernanda's monologue, which quotes other members of the family at some length and asks a question no one ever asked her, "Good morning, Fernanda, did you sleep well?" Since the question was never asked and no response is given, this does not constitute a full interaction, but it is as close an approach to one as occurs in the speech. Further, Fernanda quotes what others have said about her; in the later uses, the speaker will quote what others have said in his presence but not necessarily directly to or about him. Of course, all these quotations, interactions, and dialogues erupt in the sentence without quotation marks or other indicators (the sections italicized in the translation of "The Handsomest Drowned Man in the World" are not italicized in the original). And the obvious question is what purpose their presence serves.

Specific purposes vary from context to context, but the general object of the device is to create a sense of some immediate action while reducing the number of characters on stage or eliminating the individuality of characters to make them representative of a community. "Blacamán the Good, Vendor of Miracles" reduces us to two very similar characters, Blacamán the Good and Blacamán the Bad, though multitudes of others rush past or cluster about, and only Blacamán the Good speaks, telling his story in the first person. "The Last Voyage of the Ghost Ship" reduces us to a single nameless character whose story is related by an omniscient narrator and who interacts only with the ghost ship, his mother, a boatman, and the townspeople who beat him up. "The Handsomest Drowned Man in the World" reduces the named characters to one, Esteban, the drowned man, and uses an omniscient narrator who adopts the perspectives of the people of the village in order to render a divided, but finally communal, imagination, shifting from the children, to the men, the women, the young women, and the oldest woman to unite them finally, men and women, in a common awakening to "the narrowness of their dreams" and a common resolve to make everything "different from then on."[1] The effect is to keep us locked inside the consciousness of a single character or community and to vary the rhetorical surface without allowing any other characters to assume an independent existence, separate from the all-embracing, all-consuming perspective adopted within the narrative.

The method communicates a very peculiar and particular obsessiveness, well illustrated in the difference between these stories and "A Very Old Man with Enormous Wings," written with the omniscient narrator, sentential management, and structural arrangement of *One Hundred Years of Solitude*. In that story, as in "The Handsomest Drowned Man in the World," an odd personage occupies the central place, a very old man with enormous wings who may be either a fallen angel or merely a winged Norwegian and who is just as unlikely and physically impossible as a beautiful drowned man. But both his fate and his relationship to other characters are very different from those in the later stories. Discovered in his backyard by Pelayo (who had been throwing into the sea Tobías's crabs from "The Sea of Lost Time"), he is first wondered at by Pelayo and Elisenda, his wife, who "interpret" him as a castaway by skipping over "the inconvenience of the wings" (158; 12); he is next identified as an angel by the wise old neighbor woman resembling the aunt of García Márquez who, as town consultant on mysteries, at once identified an oddly shaped hen's egg brought for her inspection as a basilisk's egg and ordered it burned. (The

1. Except for "The Sea of Lost Time," "Death Constant beyond Love," and "The Incredible and Sad Tale of Innocent Eréndira and her Heartless Grandmother," which appear in *Innocent Eréndira,* English translations of these stories appear in *Leafstorm and Other Stories,* p. 153. *La Increíble y triste historia de la cándida Eréndira y de su abuela desalmada: siete cuentos* (Mexico City: Hermes, 1972), p. 56.

wise old woman recommends clubbing the angel to death.) The angel is gawked at, investigated by the church with proper suspicion, made a carnival attraction, tormented by the curious who flock to see him, and then loses his celebrity to a woman turned into a spider, but not before he has enriched Elisenda and Pelayo, in whose house he stays, an intolerable inconvenience and a companion to their child, until he finally grows back his feathers and flies away. The story's splendor is the implicit contrast between what we expect angels to be like and what this one is, with his strong sailor's voice, his unbearable smell, parasite-infested wings, diet of eggplant mush, and clumsy first attempts at flight: this is an angel as buzzard.

Some of the changes worked in García Márquez's language by *One Hundred Years of Solitude* are evident in the differences between the opening of this story and that of "The Sea of Lost Time." The first paragraph of "The Sea of Lost Time" takes us from January when "the sea was growing harsh [and] beginning to dump its heavy garbage on the town" to the year when Mr. Herbert came and, instead of changing for the worse, the sea "grew smoother and more phosphorescent" and finally gave off "a fragrance of roses" (60; 23). That beautiful oddity ends the paragraph. In "A Very Old Man with Enormous Wings," the first sentence makes a temporal loop like that which begins the novel, moving from the third day of rain to Pelayo's throwing the crabs in the sea, back to the night before and the newborn child's temperature, attributed to the stench. As should be evident, that sentence packs in several relationships, several times, and the thoughts as well as the actions of the characters. The phosphorescence and the garbage of the sea have been transferred to the sands of the beach, which "glimmered like powdered light" and "had become a stew of mud and rotten shellfish" (157; 11). The images are more specific. And the paragraph ends not with a beautiful but with a comic, paradoxical oddity, a very old man who could not get up, "impeded by his enormous wings." Other stylistic affinities with *One Hundred Years of Solitude* appear in hyperbole that causes a contradiction, the old man's wings are "forever entangled in the mud"; in absurd lists, the letters the priest receives from Rome, the ailments of those who seek cures from the angel, the ridiculous miracles he does perform; the quick movement between objective description and analysis and commentary by the narrator; the long period of time covered but only tentatively sketched by the story, from the recent birth of the child until sometime after he begins school; the finality and release of the conclusion, the angel came, and the angel went, without causation.

The difference between this story and the others from 1968 is that here, although the angel is central and every event bears on him, on his appearance, behavior, identity, fate, or effects, our attention to the angel is frequently interrupted by shifts of focus to other characters, sometimes named, often described at length, and by the obtrusiveness of the narrator, who is both at one with and apart from the characters in the story, like the narrator of *One Hundred Years of Solitude*. When Father Gonzaga enters, for example, we are treated to his suspicions of the angel, his observations upon him, his sermon to the gathered townspeople, and his promise to seek advice from higher authorities. A few pages later, there appears a synopsis of his correspondence about the angel, and in another few pages, the waning of the angel's popularity cures Father Gonzaga of his insomnia, and he disappears from the narrative. The full history of the woman who was turned into a spider for having disobeyed her parents constitutes another episode and provides a similar distraction, as does the imaginative excess of the ailments suffered by those who seek the angel's help and the cures he provides, the blind man who stayed blind but grew three new teeth, the leper whose sores sprouted sunflowers, the paralytic who did not recover the use of his limbs but almost won the lottery. Such details call attention to themselves, rather than to their cause, and the difference from García Márquez's management of hyperbole in "The Handsomest Drowned Man in the World" is instructive.

If episodic structure and narrative commentary distract us from the angel, everything in the other story keeps us focused on the drowned man. Even the inevitable description of the village, delayed until the third paragraph, is contained within a paragraph that begins and ends with how the villagers determined that the drowned man was a stranger. The sea itself, with which the story as inevitably begins, is no more than that through which the drowned man floats to shore, mistaken by the children first for an enemy ship, then for a whale. The drowned man is re-markable for his size to the children and for his weight to the men who carry him to the nearest house and hypothesize that it was perhaps in the nature of some drowned men to "keep on growing after death" (146; 49), like the boy in "The Third Resignation." Only when the women have removed the mud and scraped off the remora with fish scalers is his beauty discovered in a series of superlatives that link inextricably the appearance of the drowned man and the minds of those who observe him: "Not only was he the tallest, strongest, most virile, and best built man they had ever seen, but even though they were looking at him there was no room for him in their imagination" (147; 50). The superlatives continue, but they are very simple superlatives: the shoes of the man with the biggest feet will not fit, nor will the pants of the tallest man, nor the shirts of the fattest. The author's hold on Esteban is so secure that the reader scarcely notices the oddity of Esteban's exchange with the lady of the house as he declines to accept the chair that she is terrified he will break. This exchange takes place only in the imagination of the women sitting around him and is part of the transformation of their awe and passion into pity. Humanized, first by being named and then by speaking, Esteban becomes more immediate, more present, both to the women and to us. But why not use quotation marks? Partly because it is not necessary to use them, partly because García Márquez was practicing getting along without them, and partly because they would be disruptive. The sudden dialogue in the middle of a sentence or paragraph is an extension of that technique of *One Hundred Years of Solitude* in which, in the middle of a long paragraph, some properly identified person says something in properly punctuated speech. Here the characters are nameless save for Esteban and are divided into "the men" and "the women." As a result, a shift into unmarked speech can be assigned without difficulty or hesitation to the appropriate group. The two short sentences in quotation marks and separate paragraphs, "He has the face of someone named Esteban" and '"Praise the Lord," they sighed. "He's ours,"' obviously merit the attention that separation secures for them (148, 52; 150, 53).

More than "A Very Old Man with Enormous Wings,"

which chronicles the cruelty of simple folk in their treatment of any out-of-the-way creature, "The Handsomest Drowned Man in the World" seems an optimistic tale for children in the new solidarity the drowned man creates among the villagers and the new determination for the future he bequeaths them, though it is elaborated only in fantasy. It makes the impossible real, in the figure of an oversize, beautiful drowned man, and it makes the possible strange, in an event that so galvanizes a community as to transform it forever. But it is the only fiction by García Márquez that is turned inside out by a later work. The later work is, of course, *The Autumn of the Patriarch*. Like Esteban, the patriarch has the huge size of a drowned man, must be scaled of underwater creatures to be readied for burial, and was too large, according to the history books, to get through doors. All his children were premature, "seven-monthers," and Esteban's too-small pants are those of a "seven-monther"; (the translation has "undersized child"; Rabassa had not seen the unfinished novel) (151; 54). Finally, devastatingly, as we are told that memories of Esteban will, so the belief in the patriarch has held his nation together for generations. If the flashes forward were not enough, there are unsettling recollections of "Big Mama's Funeral" in "the most splendid funeral they could conceive of" for their drowned man and the heartwarming assignment of relatives to Esteban "so that through him all the inhabitants of the village became kinsmen" (152; 55). The story should probably still be read as optimistic and therefore a tale for children, its hopefulness tempered even in its own conclusion by the extravagance of the villagers' fantasy that the scent of their rose gardens on the high seas will bring the captains of great ocean liners down from the bridge to point out to the insistent passengers in fourteen languages "over there, where the sun's so bright that the sunflowers don't know which way to turn, yes, over there, that's Esteban's village" (154; 56). But the parallels suggest García Márquez's awareness of the ambiguity of the power of illusion.

If we had any doubts about his awareness of that ambiguity, "Blacamán the Good, Vendor of Miracles" would dispel them. Blacamán is a species, though he has a very particular history, and his division into Blacamán the Good and Blacamán the Bad, realizing the potential relationship between Esteban and the patriarch, is, the story suggests, a trick of rhetoric. Reappearing in "Innocent Eréndira" playing Blacamán the Bad's opening trick of asking for a serpent in order to test his antidote on himself, Blacamán finally becomes a legend in "Death Constant beyond Love," as Laura Farina's father sighs of Senator Onésimo Sánchez (who of course figured in "Innocent Eréndira"), "C'est le Blacamén de la politique" (87; 63). But Blacamán had already become a legend in his own story.

For Blacamán, Good or Bad, is the immortal huckster, the con man who never dies. If Blacamán the Good possesses the impossible ability to resurrect the dead and to live forever, he uses it only to keep Blacamán the Bad alive in his tomb "as long as I'm alive, that is, forever" (184; 14). And his greatest con may be persuading the reader to believe that he is Blacamán the *Good*. When the story opens, the unnamed speaker is describing seeing "him" for the first time. Not until the third of the interminable paragraphs does the speaker name Blacamán, whom he qualifies as Blacamán the Bad, while he himself is Blacamán the Good. Playing on our sympathies and perhaps our memory of the first and second Adams, the second Blacamán persuades us that he deserves to be called "the Good" because of his sufferings and his miraculous powers, gained through suffering. The two Blacamáns have separate histories, but both histories have political overtones, and both seem to be cyclic. Blacamán the Bad deceived the marines and gave the viceroys he embalmed a look of such authority as to enable them to continue ruling after their deaths; Blacamán the Good puts his audiences to sleep "with the techniques of a congressman" (180; 91) and blithely remakes history with the inscription on Blacamán the Bad's tombstone. While the story ends with Blacamán the Good at his apogee, he has related both Blacamán the Bad's fall and his earlier prosperity, while his own reappearance in "Innocent Eréndira" suggests that by then he too may have fallen on evil times.

A simple tale of the turning of fortune's wheel, the rhetoric is the richest since "Big Mama's Funeral" and for the same reason: to erect a barrier of words between the protagonist and the reader, to achieve distance through stylization. In the opening sentence, the details of the still nameless Blacamán the Bad's dress are so thoroughly specified that he almost disappears: "From the first Sunday I saw him he reminded me of a bullring mule, with his white suspenders that were backstitched with gold thread, his rings with colored stones on every finger, and his braids of jingle bells, standing on a table by the docks of Santa Maria del Darien in the middle of the flasks of specifics and herbs of consolation" (171; 83). When at the end of that sentence, we suddenly hear Blacamán's voice, the voice is not a personal one, but the eternal voice of the sideshow barker. The sort of detail that distracts us briefly from the angel in "A Very Old Man with Enormous Wings" is deployed here throughout; sometimes the details seem altogether meaningless. Why should Blacamán the Bad smuggle Blacamán the Good "disguised as a Japanese"? Sometimes they are disquietingly meaningful, as in the description of the Blacamáns' flight: "the more lost we became, the clearer the news reached us that the marines had invaded the country under the pretext of exterminating yellow fever and were going about beheading every inveterate or eventual potter they found in their path, and not only the natives, out of precaution, but also the Chinese, for distraction, the Negroes, from habit, and the Hindus, because they were snake charmers" (177; 88). Before the sentence ends, it has incorporated economic exploitation and an allusion to Carpentier's *Kingdom of This World* in the gringos' belief that the natives of the Caribbean have the power to change form. Such details shift us, in the very act of reading, from the text to the world outside the text, the fundamental act of satire.

"The Last Voyage of the Ghost Ship," apart from the management of its sentence, is much simpler rhetorically and, to my mind, altogether impenetrable. From the speaker's opening "Now they'll see who I am," the story unfolds the town's disbelief in the ghost ship that the boy sees on March nights and that at first he himself thought was an illusion, though years of watching it destroy itself on the shoals have now emboldened him to say "Now they'll see who I am," as he saves the ship from its customary destruction and guides it into the town, running it aground in front of the church where he has the pleasure of watching the townspeople contemplate openmouthed the largest ocean liner in the world, with its name *Halalcsillag* engraved in iron letters and the waters of the sea of

death dripping down its side. With a little guidance, anyone can tell stories in a sentence, but the tale's real
achievement is its evasion of interpretation by presenting
so many possibilities and denying any evidence that binds
the story to one. The allegorical structure is the human
power to make real and visible to others what was at first
only a private vision, discounted and ridiculed. And it
applies equally well to art, politics, religion, science, and
any human endeavor that originates in an individual and
ends by making a difference to others. While such en-
deavors may begin in the individual's desire for identity
and recognition and even in hostility and rage, they end by
making something independent of the person in whom
they originate, who may take pleasure in the effect and
materiality of what he has made, but who is finally irrele-
vant to it, which finds its existence in the effect it has on
others and which is finally only itself. In other fictions of
this period, "Death Constant beyond Love" and "The
Handsomest Drowned Man in the World," ocean liners
have figured as emblems of power, prosperity, and freedom that pass and do not enter those dismal villages, but
shed a little radiance as they go; and this liner is evidently
Scandinavian, like the Norwegian with wings. But if it is
easy and appealing to make the boy an artist and his ship a
book, it is just as easy to make him a politician and his ship
a revolution. So perhaps it is best to leave them as a boy
and a ship.

Why is the story told in a single sentence that is not for
a moment either awkward or unclear? Apart from the desire to experiment for the patriarch's sake, the single sentence suggests the unity of the boy's obsession, from its
casual origin when he himself is skeptical of the ship's
existence, through the bitter single-mindedness he de-
velops when others resist belief and beat him for his, to the
astonishment and vindication he feels when a mystery
snuffs out the harbor buoys and he is able to guide, control, and present the ship to the town. That a mystery
snuffs out the buoys, giving the boy power over the ship,
seems to be an acknowledgment of the mysterious sources
of human creative power. We can point to the biographical
origins and see the results, but we have no idea how it was
done, even if the achievement is our own. Pointing out
that "The Last Voyage of the Ghost Ship" originates in a

simile at the end of *Leafstorm*, "the coffin is floating in the light as if they were carrying off a dead ship to be buried" (142) affords no explanation at all of the art of García Márquez.

In "Death Constant beyond Love" and "The Incredible and Sad Story of Innocent Eréndira and her Heartless Grandmother," García Márquez's manner makes another revolution, combining some ingredients from the mode of the fictions prior to *One Hundred Years of Solitude*, folding in certain of the later rhetorical practices, and baking them in a moderate oven with even heat to serve up something else again. "Death Constant beyond Love" is a very short story, "Innocent Eréndira" a very long one, and though they share certain characteristics, they are very different with respect to purpose and degree of realism. "Death Constant beyond Love," for the first time in a long time, tells the realistic story of a man in a stressful, but thoroughly recognizable situation. "Innocent Eréndira" is in large part a political allegory, as the other is not, that makes strange and therefore endurable the too-possible predicament of the heroine, prostituted by her grandmother. The stories share, however, a new spaciousness, a movement away from the compression of *One Hundred Years of Solitude* and the later stories, effected by a minute, slow development of relationships among characters, articulated through dialogue, properly punctuated and paragraphed. This attention to the interaction of characters is closer to the earlier fictions than to the later and is accompanied by a reduction in the rapidity with which episodes succeed one another and by a reduction in the seeming independence of episodes or phrases from the rest of the rhetorical surface. At the same time, García Márquez does not abandon his smuggler's tricks but uses his characteristic imagery, paradoxes, and ironies to create complex characters who are neither purely victims nor merely objects of satire. Eréndira's grandmother pushes hard against this generalization, but I will argue that it holds. Resembling in their complexity the characters of *One Hundred Years of Solitude*, these characters are no longer divided from the reader by the multiplication of episode but are instead clearly visible in their frailty and their final responsibility for what becomes of them. In the middle of weaving the patriarch's tapestry of illusions of reality, García Márquez seems to be turning the web over to the side of show where life is "arduous and ephemeral" and love is "contaminated by the seeds of death."

Although it is not a political allegory, "Death Constant beyond Love" contains a significant political component through its protagonist, Senator Onésimo Sánchez, a hardworking, corrupt senator on his quadrennial campaign tour through the desert towns of his district. The story begins, as García Márquez's stories often do when he is about to unravel the self-serving illusions of politics, with a paragraph that summarizes the action in advance. To its representation of that common syndrome of the happily married, forty-two-year-old man terrified of time, finding a new intensity through an illicit and temporally circumscribed passion for a much younger woman, the author adds a literal death sentence: the senator has been told by his doctors that he will die in six months, and the senator has told no one. Now more than ever a disbeliever in the illusions he purveys, the senator not only accepts the eternal absence of the cardboard vision of progress, brick houses and an ocean liner moving past, that his men set up to provide a climax to his speech of promises, but he also recognizes that his own continued political existence depends on the absence of that progress and the continued collaboration between him and those in the town who live off the poverty of the rest. The certainty of death provides a final disillusionment, and the usually chaste senator accepts the offer of Laura Farina's favors in exchange for a favor to her father that he has been refusing for years. But it is only a shift of illusions. Death is more constant than love, and while Blacamán the Bad may have succeeded in deceiving death by feigning lovesickness, the senator cannot.

One Hundred Years of Solitude can be accused of sentimentalizing "love" in that harping on the absence of love implies that its presence would change things in an important way. Since the characters in the novel embrace most of the forms love takes among human beings, but the narrator tells us that only the child with a pig's tail is engendered in love, to associate with solitude all the other shapes that love takes seems naive and sentimental. Fortunately for the novel, the author is a little sentimental but

83

not naive: the only passion he grants the name of love issues in the child that ends the line, eaten by ants. So much for the ability of love to change the world: it does, but not in the way we might desire. For the senator, facing death, love is doubtless more comforting than his politics, as the physical position he adopts indicates, curled up like a child, his head on Laura Farina's shoulder, his face in her armpit. He is never represented making love to her, though it is pleasant to observe that the author's sexual technique has improved since *One Hundred Years of Solitude:* no longer merely explosive or playful, it has become slow, luxurious, and gentle.

Stylistically, the slowing of García Márquez's pace emerges in the paradoxes articulated by the narrator in the first paragraph (between the appearance of the town and the possibility of it containing someone able to change another's life, between the name of the town, its roselessness, and the rose the senator wears) and in his management in the second paragraph of a typical burlesque list. The usual elements are there, but separated by "real" time they no longer come at us pell-mell: "The carnival wagons had arrived in the morning. Then came the trucks with the rented Indians who were carried into the towns in order to enlarge the crowds at public ceremonies. A short time before eleven o'clock, along with the music and rockets and jeeps of the retinue, the ministerial automobile, the color of strawberry soda, arrived" (83–84; 59). Because this story is about politics, love, and venality, there are three kinds of flying creatures in it: the paper birds released during the campaign speech that fly out to sea; the paper butterfly the senator makes while talking to the town leaders and tosses into the fan's air current, which carries it out of the room and flattens it against the wall in the next room where Laura Farina, failing to scrape it off, is told by a drowsy guard that it is painted on the wall; and, after the town leaders have left, the thousands of banknotes flapping in the air when Laura Farina walks into the senator's room, to be told as he turns off the fan, "'You see,' he said, smiling, 'even shit can fly'" (90; 66). Widely spaced, these parallel actions possess different symbolic implications appropriate to their different degrees of possibility and instance the use of the hyperbolic and the impossible in a realistic context that is stretched but not violated by them.

Stylistically, in its disposition of individual elements, "Innocent Eréndira" resembles "Death Constant beyond Love," but it differs in its selection of elements and in their relation to verisimilitude. The story of "Innocent Eréndira" is tabloid stuff: girl prostituted by grandmother conspires to murder grandmother. Girl escapes, the lover she persuaded to carry out the murder is taken into custody. From the first appearance of a nameless, ungrandmothered Eréndira in "The Sea of Lost Time" to the story's elaboration of a two-page incident in *One Hundred Years of Solitude*, however, it is clear that García Márquez is interested in forced prostitution as a metaphor for economic exploitation, foreign or domestic, but more often foreign. Like economic exploitation, prostitution, even when forced, cannot occur without the acquiescence of the victim whom it corrupts by offering only an uneasy choice between poverty and dishonor. As in "The Last Voyage of the Ghost Ship," Innocent Eréndira's prostitution works more as metaphor than as allegory since its conclusion offers too many possible readings to make an altogether successful allegory. The allegorist may decide that Eréndira's murder of her grandmother and flight with the gold represent nationalization, the return to the people of the profits of their oppression; or he may decide that murder and flight represent nationalization through the revolution, a necessary violence if the profits are to be returned to the people, but what is he to do with the disappearance of the people, never to be heard of again? Or the separation of the people from their revolutionary instrument, Ulises, whom they abandon? The committed allegorist will manage somehow, but it seems more sensible to regard the story as Eréndira's, whose history touches intermittently but not continuously another level of meaning.

Eréndira's history charts a course from pure passivity to her family tyrant, through resistance forcibly overcome by the first man to whom she is sold, rescue by the church that gives her a momentary happiness, lost when she is restored by her habit of obedience to her grandmother and followed by a mounting hatred for the old woman that issues in a failed attempt to elope with Ulises, the eventual murder of the grandmother by Ulises, and Eréndira's escape. Eréndira's transformation from passivity to resistance is not benign. Related as it is, with even less access

than is usual in García Márquez to the internal consciousness of characters (a feature made necessary perhaps by
the ugliness of the material with which he is working), the
gradual welling up of resistance in Eréndira entails the loss
of all positive affect and the submersion of all other feelings
by the desire to rid herself of her oppressor. Pitiable as a
victim, she is in large part responsible for her own submission and only less so for the deformation her character
undergoes.

As to her grandmother, she too is a victim, though one
we hold fully responsible for what becomes of her. And
there would seem to be little to humanize that great white
whale who gives orders in her sleep, procures a letter from
Senator Onésimo Sánchez testifying to her high moral
character so that she can prostitute her granddaughter
unmolested, survives arsenic sufficient to exterminate a
generation of rats and an exploding piano, and bleeds
green, the color of our money, when she finally succumbs
to Ulises's knife. But she has determination and her
memories. She subdues a revolt of inconsiderate men who
do not want to line up again at nine the next morning but
want Eréndira now, and she comforts Eréndira with the
prospect that the wealth she is now gaining will protect her
from the mercies of men later in life and will make her
independent with a house of her own. Even in her old age,
faded and fat, it "could have been said that she had been
the most beautiful woman in the world" (26; 125); she
dreams dreams and suffers nostalgia, though the longest
of her dreams ends with her killing a man in a context
that resembles "The Woman Who Came at Six o'Clock."

As in most of García Márquez's fictions, the rhetorical
surface is made up of a mosaic of elements from hetero-
geneous sources. The phrase "I'm the domestic mail"
(13; 110) was first said by a man García Márquez met in El
Chocó in 1954, and Ulises's oranges with diamonds inside
them may derive from an image García Márquez invented
on the same trip—that if bananas were planted in El Chocó,
they would grow with grains of platinum inside them.[2]
The missionary nuns' theft of Eréndira alludes to Vargas
Llosa's *The Green House*, and Ulises's face of a traitor angel

2. *Crónicas y reportajes* (Medellín, Colombia: Oveja Negra, 1978), pp.
154–55.

seems to allude to Asturias's Miguel Angel Face (Cara de Angel) in *El señor presidente*, perhaps as restitution for the many unkind things García Márquez has said about Asturias as man and as artist and perhaps as coals of fire for Asturias's accusing García Márquez of plagiarism. Alvaro Cepeda Samudio reappears driving the truck for which his physiognomy ordained him, and the narrator in the first person claims to have got the end of the story of Eréndira from Rafael Escalona, one of his own characters who is also a contemporary popular singer.

The odd appearance of the first-person narrator in "Innocent Eréndira," briefly introducing himself and his source for a few sentences before disappearing under the surface again, suggests the importance to these stories of knowing the ending before the story begins to be told. The common effectiveness in the management of closure shared by these tales no longer depends on annihilating the world or the fiction. Instead, finality is achieved though ends are left open: we do not know where the man with wings or Eréndira goes, but they do escape; we do not know what will become of Esteban's village or what will be done with the ghost ship; Blacamán lives forever, and only the senator conclusively dies, weeping with rage. Congruent with the degree of artifice in the fictions, the endings confirm the fictitiousness of all endings save one but suggest with a chastened hopefulness the continuing, transforming power of ideas.

V. IN THE LABYRINTH OF THE MINOTAUR—WITHOUT THESEUS: THE AUTUMN OF THE PATRIARCH

> This is the wandering wood, this *Errours den,*
> A monster vile, whom God and man does hate:
> Therefore I read beware. Fly fly (quoth then
> The fearfull Dwarfe:) this is no place for living men.
>
> Spenser, *Faerie Queene*, I, i, 13

As readers of *The Autumn of the Patriarch* well know, the purpose of the novel, unlike its style, is transparent: to embody and to annihilate the figure of the dictator as he has flourished principally in Latin America but also throughout the historical past into the present. As with *One Hundred Years of Solitude*, the idea for the novel was with the author long before it came to be written: he has placed it in an experience in Caracas, January 1958. Waiting with other journalists in Miraflores Palace for the end of a meeting concerning the successor to Pérez Jiménez, he saw an official abruptly leave the meeting with a machine gun under his arm, his boots plastered with mud, crossing the antechamber as if he were fleeing. A seven years' labor of close-stitching, the author has said that it is so intricately worked that there were times when he realized he had forgotten something and could not find a place to put it, so there may be some significance to the atypical dust-jacket photo of the usually smiling García Márquez on both English and Spanish editions: head down, hand in hair, scowling, behind a desk and what appears to be a typewriter but may be a tape recorder, the image of a writer in agony.

Somewhere along the way, García Márquez abandoned the dictator's monologue as too confining and adopted the shifting voices of the stories of 1968, giving up his earlier vocation of magician for that of ventriloquist. With the monologue went the popular tribunal before which he was to deliver it, and García Márquez sought no substitute to represent the power of the people to make revolutions. Instead, he enclosed the dictator within the voice of the people who find him dead without having themselves brought about that death. The opening pages of the six unnumbered chapters cover a period of twenty-four hours in which the people discover the body on

Monday morning (chapter one), look for evidence to iden-
tify the corpse of which they are properly suspicious because this is the second time he has been found (chapter
two), fail to find that evidence (chapter three), implement
plans for reassembling and embalming the body and wait
for the fulfillment of the predicted prodigies that were
supposed to accompany his death (chapter four), finish
scaling, washing, powdering, paraffining, and rougeing
the corpse shortly before nightfall, when "we" the people
suddenly become a smaller, more exclusive group
gathered in the cabinet room around the long walnut table,
who issue calls "for the unity of all against the despotism
of centuries so we could divide up the booty of his power
in equal parts"[1] and who lay plans to announce the death
by degrees in a series of medical bulletins before tolling the
cathedral bells on Tuesday (chapter five). Finally, the dictator is laid out on the banquet table in the ballroom, cook-
ing slowly through the middle of the night while those in
the cabinet room discuss the final bulletin and troops take
up their positions throughout the city; then it is dawn, it is
Tuesday, it is a national holiday, and the jubilation begins
at the end of the chapter (chapter six). Observing the uni-
ties of time, place, and action, the frame of the novel has
the additional but eerie classical nicety that it recapitulates
an action we already know, since precisely the same stages
in the same language from preparation to jubilation have
already been traversed in the first chapter when the patriarch died the first time. Nor is it comforting to find a
lieutenant who does not know what all the mysterious
preparations mean, laughing that "the dead man must
have come back to life" (204; 220).

Within this frame, the novel relates the history of the
patriarch from his conception to his death along a
chronological spine that extends from the beginning of his
autumn to its end, the vertebrae composed of a single
character or pair of characters who dominate that chapter
of the patriarch's personal, political life. For the first half of
the novel, there are no links between the character and
episode dominant in one chapter and those dominant in

1. *The Autumn of the Patriarch,* trans. Gregory Rabassa (New York:
Harper and Row, 1976), p. 157. *El otoño del patriarca* (Barcelona: Plaza y
Janés, 1975), p. 169.

the next, but in the last three chapters, the outcome of one episode serves to introduce the character who will dominate the next. The second and third chapters differ from the rest in that the second is divided evenly between an earlier period and a later character important to the patriarch, and in the third episodes of a particular kind rather than a character are the principal focus. Throughout, the patriarch reacts and is acted upon, rarely initiating action and never having full control over the outcome of events except through make-believe, as when he changes night to day or the endings of soap operas. The lifeline to which the reader grapples for the course of the novel is thus reeled out as follows: At the beginning of his autumn, when the patriarch still feels menaced by death, he has the good luck to find a double, Patricio Aragones, to make his public appearances for him and to be assassinated for him in his first, false death, after which he reasserts his authority (chapter one). Then the century of peace begins, as do the "noisy times," named for the noise made about projects to be performed that were never completed, and, imitating his double's pining for beauty queens, the dictator falls in love with Manuela Sánchez, whose image passes through walls to him as death herself will. She touches his hand when the comet passes and disappears during the eclipse that he arranges in hope of a repeat performance (chapter two). Still mourning Manuela Sánchez's disappearance, he is luckily distracted by a cyclone that destroys the city, and in the midst of the corruption that ensues with the relief supplies, he is reminded of the problem with the children, his drastic solution to which leads him into serious political difficulties, a succession of coup and assassination attempts, eventuating in the suspicion that he has been betrayed by "the comrade of my life," General Rodrigo de Aguilar, who arrives for dinner with a vengeance (chapter three). On the death of his mother, the miracle of the shroud and the body that though rotten in life does not decay in death convinces him that she should be canonized, and the indomitable Eritrean Demetrious Aldous arrives from Rome as devil's advocate to uncover the fraud of the poor, stuffed mother, mangled by taxidermists for the profit of sellers of relics. Since the Holy See refuses to canonize Bendición Alvarado, her civil sainthood is proclaimed, all the religious are expelled from the country, and church property is confiscated. As the religious file naked out of the country, the patriarch's eye is caught by one novice, whose name he murmurs, and who is kidnapped for him in Jamaica, brought in a crate, kept in naked captivity for a year until the patriarch discovers the terror of love made without clothes for the first time in his life (chapter four). Leticia Nazareno teaches him to read and write, drags him to the marriage altar where she gives birth, brings back the church and enriches her kin, to the distress of the ruling families whose customary hegemony is infringed, runs up enormous debts, and, Jezebel that she is, is eaten by dogs with her son in the marketplace. To find the perpetrators of this heinous deed, José Ignacio Saenz de la Barra appears and begins to send the heads of the guilty in sacks to the patriarch, as Joab received the heads of the seventy sons of Ahab, and, as authority but not power slips away from the patriarch, the hundredth anniversary of his reign is celebrated (chapter five). Progress within order continues under the direction of Saenz de la Barra's French torturers, rationalists who are therefore methodical, until an uprising against Saenz de la Barra occurs, which the patriarch turns into a triumph for himself. The nation's debts are enormous, its material progress illusory, its leader incapacitated by senility for everything except staying in power, but he dies in his sleep in the wrong room and the wrong dress, not fulfilling the prediction that he himself read in the waters of the sybil's basin and not corresponding to the description of the way he was found either the first or the second time (chapter six).

The earlier periods of the patriarch's history emerge in the course of this narrative, with his childhood and first amorous experiences juxtaposing the death of his mother in chapter four, his accession to power with British help after the overthrow of Lautaro Muñoz delayed until chapter six, his consolidation of power through the liquidation of the remaining federalist generals in chapter two, his personal government with Saturno Santos as his only bodyguard in chapter three, his summons of the gringos to quell civil unrest, disguised as a request for assistance against an imaginary plague that becomes real and leads the patriarch on a tour distributing the salt of health (chapter six). Under the gringo occupation, the patriarch's mother moves to her suburban mansion, and authority is taken out of his hands, but the gringos are finally frightened away by a real epidemic, restore him to his "nigger whorehouse," and decorate him with the badge of the good neighbor. Rid of them, he accumulates fantastic wealth (all this in chapter two), and the double turns up in chapter one to begin his autumn. García Márquez winds into these episodes in a variety of ways, sometimes through what the patriarch remembers or does not remember, what his mother remembers or tells him, what "we" remember or what is told in the banned memoirs of some ambassador, but the effect is to hold off certain explanations of events until the close so that origins and endings can be brought together, and to provide a clear picture of the patriarch in vigorous action in the first half of the novel that contrasts sharply with his decay in the latter half, while the image of the pitiable child is safely trapped in the center, next to his mother. It is almost, but not quite, possible for the reader to reconstruct the novel in chronological order, phrase by phrase, for such mysteries remain as the guards who fled in panic, leaving their Sunday lunch on the tables of the first page.

Cementing the disorderly but purposive progress of the dictator is a seemingly inexhaustible variety of recurring motifs, some of which evoke the passing of time, others its stasis: the sale of the sea, the shad scales breaking out on the patriarch's body, his herniated testicle and hidden honey, Rubén Darío, his nightly routine of locking himself up, the cripples, lepers, and blindmen in the rosebushes, the endless succession of ambassadors, the proliferation of cows and seven-month bastards, the little glass ball of power rolling in his hand. Throughout, the patriarch's adventures reenact the deeds of other great heroes: the cult of Eva Perón in Argentina; the mother of a Bolivian president who said that if she had known her son was going to be president, she would have had him learn to read and write; the permanent display of Lenin; Napoleon's hand inside his coat and his rank of artillery lieutenant; the long death of Salazar; Caesar's murder in the Roman senate; Somoza's dairy, earthquake, and gringo occupation; the feminine hands of Stalin; and a nameless man, marked with the sign of solitude, who seeks the patriarch's aid in wiping out conservative regimes from Alaska to Patagonia but only convinces the patriarch that he is so good for nothing he need not even be kept under surveillance, whom the reader may recognize as Colonel Aureliano Buendía. The pervasiveness of allusion suggests one purpose of the novel: to render the dictator not as he might once have inhabited one body in one country, but as he has inhabited many bodies in many countries, for the problem presented by dictatorship is not that it happened once, but that it happens again and again and again, in barbaric nations, in civilized nations, in semicivilized nations. The fit of means to message in *The Autumn of the Patriarch* is, to put it simply and without exaggeration, perfect. To communicate concretely the quandary of dictatorship's durability, universality, and recurrence, no more effective conceit could be devised than this of a circular novel that endows the dictator with between 107 and 232 years of life and a resurrection. That hyperbole with respect to a single dictator is understatement with respect to the species, and it is the species García Márquez gives us through the particularity of the patriarch, with all the horrors of his reign heightened and rendered all too human by humor.

But however clear the author's purposes, the reader may well wonder why reading has been made so difficult for him, lost in the endless sentences of an endless paragraph, six times over, until in the sixth section, the sentence becomes the paragraph. While the patriarch may miss the sea and the songs of birds, the reader misses paragraph divisions, quotation marks, and all the other faithful typographical servants that make our lives easier without our taking any notice of them. It would be easy and probably accurate enough to say that García Márquez seeks an effect of total immersion and so has provided a full, minutely articulated, and continuous surface in which the variety of detail is to be read cumulatively as well as piece by piece. The style is difficult only if the reader reads at his conventional speed. Once he has learned to attend to the comma and the phrase as his principal units and markers, he is baffled only by his inability to remember, without notes, where he first saw the phrase or event that is now repeated and what temporal relationship holds between various epochs in the patriarch's history. The basic devices that García Márquez exploits are identical to those in *One Hundred Years of Solitude:* hyperbole, allusion, paradox, intermittent insights into the minds of characters, an omniscient narrator, perversions of chronological order, the introduction of new inventions to mark the passage of time, repetition of phrases, parallels of events, within an episodic structure in which events always have priority over analysis. And lots of sex and violence.

The different deployment of common devices in novels with a common effect of sensory overload suggests that to achieve the same fullness in the rhetorical surface in a novel with a much narrower focus, the author had to increase the simple density of that surface. *One Hundred Years of Solitude* has six generations of a family as its object; *The Autumn of the Patriarch*, a single character who may outlast six generations of any family in his domain but who is still only a single character. Apart from the ambassadors, several victims, a few generals, and Zacarías himself, there are fewer than a dozen named characters in the novel, very few of whom overlap (Patricio Aragones, the double; General Rodrigo de Aguilar, comrade of my life; Bendición Alvarado, my mother; Demetrious Aldous, the devil's advocate; Leticia Nazareno and Emanuel, wife and child; Manuela Sánchez, beloved maiden; Francisca Linero, raped newlywed; General Saturno Santos, Guajiro Indian, rival, and right-hand man; José Ignacio Saenz de la Barra, master torturer; General Lautaro Muñoz, supplanted dictator). Hundreds of others troop past or slither through, and the total population of the novel exceeds that of *One Hundred Years of Solitude* as the population of a nation exceeds that of any town within it. Naming has been reduced in part to prevent the novel from reading like a national telephone directory and in part to give us the nation as the patriarch sees it, nameless except for the very few people who are important to him. The scattered naming of ambassadors, generals, and victims lights them up momentarily before they disappear, anonymous once more, forgotten by patriarch and reader alike. (For example, a brief test: what is the name of the boy toward the end of the novel whom the patriarch is sure that he recognizes and incarcerates for twenty-two years until he realizes that he was mistaken, that he had never seen him before, and leaves incarcerated because "if he hadn't been an enemy he is now, poor man" [242; 261]? The name is familiar, the domicile known.) To adopt a narrative perspective that simultaneously hugs always to the patriarch and reaches out to include the whole nation is impossible in the tradition of the great panoramic novel from Fielding to Galdós: the protagonist disappears into the social context elaborated through independent, interlocking episodes and characters representative of diverse social strata and interests. In *The Autumn of the Patriarch,* instead of the author's having elaborated a context within which to place a range of characters and interests, the succession of perspectives, attitudes, and voices defines the context. The rapidity of movement that belonged to episodic succession in *One Hundred Years of Solitude* has been moved into the shifting perspectives within the sentence itself, the unity of which suggests the simultaneity of contradictory attitudes. The following illustration is from the last chapter, the points of view indicated in brackets:

> we had ended up not understanding what would become of us without him, what would become of our lives after him [communal meditation of the people], I couldn't conceive of the world without the man who had made me happy at the age of twelve as no other man was ever to do again since those afternoons so long ago when we would come out of school at five o'clock and [reminiscences of a former schoolgirl] he would be lying in wait by the skylights of the stables for the girls in blue uniforms with sailors' collars and a single braid thinking [omniscient narrator] mother of mine Bendición Alvarado how pretty women look to me at my age [soliloquy of dictator], he would call to us, we would see his quivering eyes, the hand with the glove with torn fingers which tried to entice us with the candy rattle from Ambassador Forbes [communal horror of schoolgirls], they all ran off frightened, all except me . . . he smelled his fingers, he made me smell them [reminiscence of schoolgirl], smell it, he told me, it's your smell [dialogue with the dictator] . . . and on the other hand he had forgotten her the second day he didn't see her climb in through the skylight of the milking stables . . . he thought of them all as the same one as he listened half-asleep in the hammock to the always identical arguments of Ambassador Streimberg who had given him an ear trumpet just like the one with the dog of his master's voice with an electrical amplifying device so that he could listen once more to the insistent plan to carry off [omniscient narrator] our territorial waters [people and the dictator, at one] and he repeated the same as always [omniscient narrator] never in a million years my dear

Stevenson, anything except the sea [dialogue of the dicta-
tor], he would disconnect the electric hearing aid so as not to
continue listening [omniscient narrator] to that loud voice of
a metallic creature who seemed to be turning the record over
to explain to him once more [dictator as third-person reflec-
tor] what had been explained to me so many times by my
own experts without any dictionary tricks that [soliloquy of
dictator] we're down to our skins, general sir [dialogue with
the experts]. (205–8; 221–24)

In this passage, we have the nation at large, the patriarch's
economic experts, two U.S. ambassadors, a schoolgirl who
pines for the patriarch and the peculiar sexual habits he
developed in his age, in addition to the patriarch himself
shifting from lascivious old man to intractable patriot. The
shifts of speaker may occur in as small a place as a single
possessive pronoun, or there may be pages of reminis-
cence punctuated largely by dialogue, as in the sections
omitted in the schoolgirl's story. Enormously flexible and
fluid, the sentence casts up objects of all kinds: the pathos
of the schoolgirl's loss and the realism of his forgetting her,
the satire of the RCA dog and the comic desperation of the
experts. The syntactic link between the sameness of the
schoolgirls and the sameness of ambassadorial arguments
generates in immediate succession two incompatible attitudes on the reader's part toward the patriarch: unsympathetic in his lovemaking, he is, not for the only time,
sympathetic as a politician.

For, like the style in which he wraps the patriarch,
García Márquez's attitude toward him is not simple. He is,
undeniably, insistently, a monster, brutal, vain, suspicious, and grasping, deformed in body as in mind, but he
is also shrewd, sentimental, populist in his convictions, a
loving son, husband, father, and a brilliant strategist. At
times, the patriarch has all the dangerous attractiveness of
an omnicompetent national father who wants to "distrib-
ute happiness and bribe death with the wiles of a soldier"
(86; 92), traveling through the country with a small retinue
of congressmen and a single bodyguard to fix sewing
machines while official delegations wait, to return strayed
husbands, to keep informed about crop figures and the
health of livestock, to punish cheating treasurers by, an
unpleasant little detail that somehow slips in, having a
butcher cut off their hands, to order manure spread at

government expense on gardens that need it for the tomatoes. It is a tempting vision, that trustworthy man who takes care of everything, even moving the rain from areas where it impeded the harvest to areas stricken by drought. Lest we yield to it, the point of view shifts from that of the patriarch and the banned memoirs of Ambassador Palmerston to that of the omniscient narrator and the people visited by the patriarch, who reveal the trail of disasters and ruined lives those visits leave in their wake, men and women assassinated because he inadvertently called them by the wrong names, the atmosphere of terror his appearance provokes, lives marked by his touch as surely as Leticia Nazareno's turned gold black and made mold grow on fruits and vegetables.

One of his finest moments is his vision of the world after he is gone: "when I finally die the politicians will come back and divide up the mess the way it was during the times of the Goths, you'll see, he said, they'll go back to dividing everything up among the priests, the gringos and the rich, and nothing for the poor, naturally, because they've always been so fucked up that the day shit is worth money, poor people will be born without an asshole, you'll see" (158–59; 171). But the context of that all too likely prediction is the dictator's unwillingness to make plans for his succession and thereby to dilute his hold on power by raising up a figure around whom alternate lines of authority will form, so creating the possibility of a world without him.

At the end of the novel, the omniscient narrator tells us that the dictator finally realizes that "he had never been master of all his power" and that he had cultivated "the solitary vice of power" to compensate for the "infamous fate" of an "incapacity for love" (250; 269). Both statements are sustained by the fiction that precedes them, but the first is a profound insight into the dependence of power, while the second seems a sentimental oversimplification, a bourgeois preference of the bliss of private, domestic life to the arduous responsibility of public life, indeed, of achievement in any kind. While it is doubtless true that the powerful and the successful often suffer in their affective lives, so do powerless failures, and the fiction itself renders obscure the meaning of an "incapacity for love" in the son of Bendición Alvarado, the husband of Leticia Nazareno, the gentle though grotesque suitor of Manuela Sánchez. The problem with the phrase, a holdover from Colonel Aureliano Buendía in *One Hundred Years of Solitude*, is that it assigns an inadequate cause to a mysterious effect and attempts to explain the ultimately inexplicable, while its purpose is to comprehend the failure of the patriarch and what he represents within a larger scheme of communal values, represented by the common lives and loves of common people. Unfortunately, it raises suspicion rather than drawing the immediate assent it is probably intended to, though it seems to be the only place where the author's wishes have triumphed over his good sense in his representation of the relations between the dictator and his people.

The novel opens as the people, following the vultures, enter the house of power. Some, the more enterprising, want to break the door down; others are unwilling to do so and find it unnecessary: the doors of the house of power open with a push and the touch of a voice, magically, as in fairy tales. For the people, the patriarch's existence is part of the natural order of things, the source of continuity and stability: "No mortal had ever seen him since the days of the black vomit and yet we knew that he was there, we knew it because the world went on, life went on, the mail was delivered, the municipal band played its retreat of silly waltzes on Saturday under the dusty palm trees and the dim street lights of the main square, and other old musicians took the places of the dead musicians in the band" (10; 9). At the end of the novel, this dependence on the idea of the patriarch has been translated into a fear of losing him: "we had even extinguished the last breath of the hopeless hope that someday the repeated and always denied rumor that he had finally succumbed to some one of his many regal illnesses would be true, and yet we didn't believe it now that it was, and not because we really didn't believe it but because we no longer wanted it to be true, we had ended up not understanding what would become of us without him, what would become of our lives after him" (205; 221). What seems to be a damning portrayal of the inertia of the people is also an insidious commentary on the irrelevance of the patriarch, necessary only as a figurehead, having nothing to do with the important continuities of daily life, and whose irrelevance to everything that really matters, the mail and Saturday music, is one of the principal reasons he and his kind manage to stay in power. In the transfer later in the novel of the government ministries from the presidential palace, the lair of power, to glass office buildings, power is explicitly separated from governance, as the patriarch remains the source of authority, while the immediate operations of government are delegated to bureaucracies of subordinate officials. Possessed of power but free of responsibility, he can tell his wife's creditors to send the bill to the government, and the people can sigh of Saenz de la Barra's acts of terror, "if he only knew." Like the Shah, he assures them he didn't, and unlike the less fortunate Persian, the people believe him.

At least, most of them do, or seem to, for the patriarch has his detractors as well as his supporters, and the novel charts the terrain of opposition without discovering a successful revolution. Rightly convinced that the people love him, the patriarch rightly fears assassination. His early ability to appear everywhere at once was neither "a privilege of his nature, as his adulators proclaimed, or a mass hallucination, as his critics said, but his luck in counting on . . . his perfect double" (15; 13–14). At his first death, he is mourned in all sincerity by a variety of figures from the old man with the Masonic salute from the federalist wars to the inconsolable fishwife, though far more join in the desecration of the body and the spoliation of the palace and the whole nation rejoices at his passing. Some, perhaps, may rejoice at the end of despotism though they grieve for the despot, a tricky maneuver of which the human heart is easily capable. But when he rises from the dead, "the same Roman candles of excitement, the same bells of jubilation that had begun celebrating his death . . . went on celebrating his immortality" (37; 37).

The most serious threats to his power come from the army, supported by the church and civilian opposition, when moved to action by his final solution to the problem of the children and by the excesses of Saenz de la Barra. The first revolt is put down by the ingenious device of a Trojan milk cart, its barrels loaded not with Greeks but with dynamite, offered selflessly to the wicked rebels who were biting the hand that fed them; the second by the unhesitating sacrifice of Saenz de la Barra and his minions. There are revolutionaries conspiring in secret, but most of them, as well as many other unfortunates, figure only as victims of Saenz de la Barra, and the single effective group, accused of the murder of Leticia Nazareno and Emanuel, has the dubious insignia of a goose quill crossed over a kitchen knife, the pen and the sword having undergone rhetorical subtraction.

The absence of a significant revolutionary movement is curious in a novel that began with the dictator before a popular tribunal and was written by an author strongly sympathetic to revolution. And I would speculate that the reason for the omission is the profound suspicion of power that the novel conveys. To gain power, revolutionaries must share some of the characteristics of the patriarch, and García Márquez may have preferred not to contaminate the idea of revolution by such propinquity. As to the popular tribunal itself, the clearest problem is that to put an effective and satisfying end to the patriarch, those who try him must possess the ability to right all the ills that flourished under him: poverty, illiteracy, great concentrations of wealth and privilege, military control, torture, censorship of the press, banning of books. Since with the possible exception of Scandinavia, there exists no such society, García Márquez would have had either to perpetrate the most startling fiction of his career or to condemn his superhuman patriarch by the merely human, inevitably flawed means of revolutionaries whom some skeptical readers might suspect to be baby patriarchs in a new dress with another rhetoric. Far better to get him offstage by natural means, begin the jubilation, and proclaim that he is gone forever, that "the uncountable time of eternity has come to an end" (251; 271).

And that, of course, is what García Márquez has done, though the reader may be more than a little puzzled as to how it is possible for "the uncountable time of eternity to come to an end." The rest of the novel has had clear reference to the things of our world, but this is one of those statements that belongs only in a book, unless it is made by the presumed source of the Book. When His trumpet sounds, we will be forced to believe it, but when his surrogates blow their horns, we do not have the same obligation. The only obligation we have is to recognize a contradiction when it leaps at us from the page. And our author is no innocent; he knows that, and pages and pages ago he told us that few of us took much interest in the comet because we believed it presaged the patriarch's death, and that death was what we were waiting for: "even the most incredulous of us were hanging on that uncommonly large death which was to destroy the principles of Christianity and implant the origins of the third testament" (79–80; 84). By itself, that messianic hope is cryptic and very puzzling. Who is our savior to be? how can there be a third testament or the end of Christianity? Christianity itself, that large compensation for the sorrows and oppressions of human existence, promises its own end at the end of time in the return of one who died, but that does not seem to be what is meant in this novel that pronounces the end of time and oppression, though not of sorrow.

Resting on that most unstable of foundations, a contradiction, the happy ending of the novel is further undermined by the exactness of the parallels between the first time the dictator was found and the second time he was found. The first time, the patriarch himself moved Patricio Aragones's body into the office and dressed him in his own uniform; the second time, some unknown hand has performed the same respectful act, for all the testimony except that of death herself in conversation with the patriarch has confirmed that he was found as predicted in the sibyl's basin. The same medical bulletins are invented; the walnut table has the same people sitting around it mouthing the same slogans about the despotism of all the centuries with the same plans to divide up the booty of power; even the troops have been moved into position. Yet we are told that this jubilation, with the same shouts, the same rockets, the same bells, brings it all to an end. It is hard to believe, nor are we meant to: we are meant instead to participate in the wish for change with the full understanding that wishes are wishes, not horses. There are fourteen federalist generals who succeed to power before the patriarch; fourteen military men of the high command whom he suspects of plotting against him; fourteen images of himself as fourteen generals repeated in mirrors on the last night of his life. In Borges's "The House of Asterion," Asterion describes his house as like no other on earth and as possessing an infinite number of doors open day and night to men and animals as well. But there is a footnote to "infinite" that reads: "The original says *fourteen*, but there is ample reason to infer that, as used by Asterion, this numeral stands for *infinite*."[2] Then there is the name of the patriarch, Zacarías, Zechariah, who, like many of the prophets, prophesies a day when "ye shall call every man his neighbor under the vine and the fig tree" and "the streets of the city shall be full of boys and girls playing in the streets thereof," images of the happiness the patriarch provides when he changes the endings of soap operas. But also in Zechariah, more rarely, there reigns in Ashdod a bastard of the race who will be cut off, and "the idols have spoken vanity, and the diviners have seen a lie, and have told false dreams." Moreover, Zechariah begins with an injunction to "Be not as your fathers, unto whom the former prophets have cried."

The contradiction that ends the novel, supported by allusion, works in two directions. Out here, where we are, reading, eternity has not ended, infinity has not run out, the prophecies have yet to be fulfilled. Where most of the world's people live, the patriarch is still in bloom, and there are shad scales on the best of polities. But when— if—the patriarch, as he corresponds to our experience, is dead, truly dead, gone forever, then it will be true to say that an eternity has ended and a new era in human existence begun, the third testament to be written in the actions of men. And, as according to "Big Mama's Funeral" it now can, Christianity itself may fade away as otiose, its mission fulfilled. Very wisely García Márquez closes the novel before we are allowed a glimpse of that paradisiacal new life, threatened as it is by the return of the old.

But what use can a novel be that ends on such a determined equivocation? It is not a novel to change the world, but it should alter, profoundly, the way its readers see the world. Because it is so dependent on the past, it has enormous predictive power, whether it predicts the long dying of Tito in Yugoslavia or the slaughter of schoolchildren by Bokassa in the Central African Empire, now again a republic, since Bokassa lacked some of the patriarch's wiles. And here and there, some of its hopefulness seems justified. Reminiscing about Anastasio Somoza, third of

2. Jorge Luis Borges, *Labyrinths*, ed. Donald A. Yates and James E. Irby (New York: New Directions, 1962), p. 138.

his line to rule Nicaragua, overthrown in 1979, and one of the models for the patriarch, the military head of state in Honduras between 1972 and 1975, Gen. Oswaldo López Arellano said that "He used to complain loudly that my land reform program would open the way to Communism, that I'd be overthrown and he'd then have to give me a job in his dairy." Who, knowing nothing of Somoza or Nicaragua, can fail to be reminded of the patriarch and his cows? Or of his longevity by the Nicaraguan leftist who said of the Somozas, "There are few of us alive who remember a time when they weren't in charge."[3] But it would be very surprising if the *Times* writer who recorded those observations had not read *The Autumn of the Patriarch*. And if he had, a perfect circle of recognitions forms: the reader of the novel recognizes in the journalism events he has already read about in the novel because the journalist, having read the novel, was struck by and so included events he had already read about in the novel. All of this occurs, appropriately enough, in the context of making land reform and the Nicaraguan revolution more palatable to the American public. To incarnate one of our culture's demons, to embody him in an exuberant and beautifully shaped fiction, and to transform forever the daily newspaper: these are not small accomplishments. To overthrow the barriers between life and art in a hermetic, self-sufficient, reflexive fiction is perhaps a greater one.

3. *New York Times*, 7 July 1980, p. A10.

VI. THE NOVELIST ON THE GRAND TOUR

—They order, said I, this matter better in France—
Sterne, *A Sentimental Journey*

Since the publication of *The Autumn of the Patriarch* in 1975, García Márquez has done a great deal of writing and relatively little publishing. According to recent interviews, he has written over eighty short stories, a novel called *Chronicle of an Expected Death*, and an account of Cuba under the U.S. blockade. All these remain unpublished, though the English reader has an illusory sense of the author's activity in the appearance of translations of works written before *The Autumn of the Patriarch*. He has also worked on adaptations for film and television of several of his short stories and earlier novels. But his most conspicuous and important activities have been political: as peripatetic propagandist for various revolutionary regimes and as diligent organizer of assistance to political prisoners throughout Latin America, financed by royalties from his novels.

The political convictions that García Márquez now articulates were fully formed in the 1950s; the only change has been in the degree and kind of activity undertaken, not in sentiments. Implicitly, explicitly, and probably correctly, García Márquez believes that socialism will ultimately prevail throughout Latin America and the world. Nondoctrinaire, he gives unqualified support to no revolutionary or socialist regime but offers enthusiastic support, suppressing most of his reservations, to many. Since in politics as in literature he is not a theorist, he has provided no convenient abstract of his thought but has scattered his attitudes and assumptions through his reportage on systems ranging from Eastern Europe and the Soviet Union to Vietnam, Cuba, Chile, and Colombia and, even more miscellaneously, through interviews. As a result, there are some undesirable gaps in the outline of his ideal socialist system on such important issues as the nature and extent of state control over private enterprise or the desirability of a perfect equality of distribution. Knowing his views on democratic socialism as it functions in Scandinavia, for example, would provide clues, but all that is known is that in Sweden he found that the whole country "smelled like a first-class rail coach." Were he asked about the instance of private enterprise, however, the notion "it depends on the situation" would almost certainly figure somewhere in the answer. He is a particularist, believing firmly that every revolution must be fitted to the particular problems, geopolitics, and culture of the nation in which it occurs and opposing firmly the imposition of foreign socialist models on Latin American revolutions. In general his position might be sketched as follows: What socialism provides that capitalism does not is social services and economic independence for the poor, in Latin America the vast majority of the population: literacy, education, health care, and a more equitable distribution of wealth. To effect these ends, expropriation of property owned by nationals and nationalization of property controlled by foreigners are to be expected, and compensation is foolish: those whose property is confiscated have long ago reaped more than they sowed. The prospect of achieving these ends by constitutional and peaceful means is illusory: the counter-revolutionaries will not allow it, and it is the counter-revolution's opposition to the revolution that causes bloodshed. The bourgeois liberties of the press, expression, assembly, and petition are desirable, as are representative government and an independent judiciary, but in any conflict in which one must choose between provision for the people's material needs and those freedoms, the choice must be made for the people's needs at the cost of those freedoms. Within a revolution, however, one may and should work quietly for the restoration of those freedoms insofar as such efforts do not jeopardize the revolution's success in more vital areas or provide grist for the revolution's enemies. (We know who *they* are.) It is a simple code and fundamentally a humanitarian one, incorporating the traditional revolutionary transfer of privilege: instead of the rich having more rights than the rest of us, the poor have more rights than the rest of us. Put less stingily, they have the right to become like the rest of us. As García Márquez once summed up the revolutionary project, he wants a revolution so that "the whole world lives better, drinks better wine, and drives better cars . . . material goods are not a natural perquisite of the bourgeoisie; they are a patrimony of humanity that the bourgeoisie has stolen. We are going to take them away from the bourgeoisie to share them among everyone."[1]

The revolution in his eyes is for the sake of living a better life and not for the sake of dying in a heroic struggle. As a corollary, for as long as he has been writing on political topics, García Márquez has made the foundation of his criticism of any system its effect on the quality of life, broadly conceived, as both the material well-being and the spirit of a place. It is not surprising to find in a Colombian piece from 1954 a cleanly set up contrast between Andagoya, an orderly, impeccable, well-built, cheerful modern town with a police inspector dying of boredom because he has nothing to do, and Andagoyita across the river, with its windowless, airless shacks with broken palm roofs, walls of discarded planks, the sordid, frightening, and disorderly habitat of animals, children, prostitutes, and workers for the U.S. company that built Andagoya to extract the Chocó's platinum. Nor is it surprising to find him begin a 1959 series on a trip "behind the iron curtain" by telling us that "the iron curtain is not a curtain, nor is it iron. It's a wooden barrier painted red and white like the signs for barbershops" and continuing by calling West Berlin an aseptic, centerless city and "enormous agency of capitalist propaganda," built "with the deliberate proposition of offering an appearance of fabulous prosperity in order to disconcert East Germany, contemplating the spectacle open-mouthed through the keyhole." But it is surprising to find him represent with the same clarity and sharpness of vision spiritual malaise in the socialist countries of Eastern Europe, to find, in the very essay on the two Berlins, a contrast between Heidelberg, the university city of West Germany, and Leipzig, the university city of East Germany, that concludes, "For us it was incomprehensible that the people of East Germany had taken over power, the means of production, commerce, banking, communications, and were nevertheless a sad people, the saddest people I had ever seen."[2] Wanting to approve what he saw, he recorded the rigidity, inefficiency, and

1. Ernesto González Bermejo, "García Márquez: La imaginación como arma política," *Triunfo* 654 (12 April 1975): 46–47.

2. Series titled "90 días en la 'Cortina de Hierro'"; "La 'Cortina de Hierro' es un palo pintado de rojo y blanco," *Cromos* 2198 (27 July 1959);

bitterness that he found without losing confidence in the attempt represented by what were then almost the only socialist countries in the world. When he did find what he had hoped to find, in Czechoslovakia, his delight emerged in a wonderfully comic paradox: trying in a cabaret on a Tuesday night to find a single "detail that would let me think we were not in a capitalist city" and not being able to.[3] When his companion found one, the runs in the singer's stockings, he protested, but understood that his friend felt the same glee he had felt when, in Nice, the most expensive beach in Europe, he had seen the city's rubbish floating in the waters where the millionaires swim.

If the fifties found him, like other Americans, in Europe, the seventies have taken him to more exotic places, to Angola to cover the Cuban assistance to Aghostino Neto, to Vietnam to look into the problem of the "boat people." But the most traumatic event of the seventies for García Márquez was the overthrow and murder in 1973 of Salvador Allende, the democratically elected Marxist president of Chile. In 1971, García Márquez had predicted that while the United States was not at present interfering in Chile, it would not allow Chile to become a socialist country, and he was profoundly skeptical of the then current hope, based on Allende's success, that socialism could be instituted by peaceful and constitutional means. Chile, he said, "is heading towards violent and dramatic events."[4] When they came, however, they seem to have been more of a shock than he was prepared for.

Nicknamed "el guatón," "the big belly," for his paunch, the bespectacled Allende had run again and again for the presidency, always a candidate, never a victor, but he was president of the Senate, widely respected as a humanitarian, doctor, and popular public figure. In 1970 his Popular Unity coalition won the presidency with 36 percent of the popular vote, and there were fears of a coup which did not materialize. The interim elections of March 1973, far from showing a diminution in Allende's support

"Berlin es un disparate," *Cromos* 2199 (3 August 1959). There is no pagination.

3. "Para una checa las medias de nailon son una joya," *Cromos* 2201 (17 August 1959).

4. Rita Guibert, *Seven Voices* (New York: Alfred A. Knopf, 1973), p. 333.

as the opposition had hoped, increased the coalition's share of the popular vote to 44 percent. With this evidence of growing popular support for an avowedly Marxist regime, the efforts at destabilization began in earnest with enormous infusions of CIA funds to support the half of the electorate, from avowed fascists to mere liberals, that wanted Allende out. On 11 September, the army moved in a carefully planned, thoroughly orchestrated, and wholly successful operation. It was a bloodbath, the proportions and ruthlessness of which astonished even the Brazilians, and it continues. Allende himself held out for six hours in the presidential palace with a submachine gun given him by Castro, and he was finally shot down by a group of officers who finished the business by smashing his face with rifle butts.

When these events occurred, García Márquez was finishing a novel about the end of dictatorship and the nature of power. After sending a seething telegram to "assassin Pinochet," assuring him that the Chilean people would not consent to be ruled by a gang of criminals in the pay of U.S. imperialism, he took the time to write a blistering essay on "The Death of Salvador Allende." Like all of García Márquez's work, it is careful, accurate, precise in its details, though, as in *The Autumn of the Patriarch*, there is little information on the methods by which the coup organized and prepared itself. The tone of the conclusion, however, confronts the pain of a contradiction that he had managed to evade in the novel:

> In that final battle, with the country at the mercy of uncontrolled and unforeseen forces of subversion, Salvador Allende was still bound by legality. The most dramatic contradiction of his life was being at the same time the congenital foe of violence and a passionate revolutionary. . . . Experience taught him too late that a system cannot be changed by a government without power. . . . His greatest virtue was following through, but fate could grant him only that rare and tragic greatness of dying in armed defense of the anachronistic booby of bourgeois law, defending a Supreme Court of Justice which had repudiated him but would legitimize his murderers, defending a miserable Congress which had declared him illegitimate but which was to bend complacently before the will of the usurpers, defending the freedom of opposition parties which had sold their souls to fascism, defending the whole moth-eaten

paraphernalia of a shitty system which he had proposed abolishing, but without a shot being fired.[5]

This language should, I think, give us pause, both in itself and as it reveals the sleight of hand by which the author has removed the need for countervailing power from *The Autumn of the Patriarch*. That removal suggests an ideal preference for getting along without the mess of power. After all, when neither of our heroes is "bound by legality," it becomes difficult to tell them apart. But the language here suggests a willingness to make oneself "a victim of his own sect to be immolated on the flames of that infinite holocaust" (Patriarch, 250; 269), to abandon humanity in the cause of humanity. As Allende did not, whose rare and tragic greatness deserves better than to have his defender carp at the value of the political institutions he died for and to deny so facilely that there are any costs when the left destroys supreme courts, congresses, and law. Allende's experience indeed suggests that social revolutions can be made through legal means only in the rarest and most fortunate of circumstances and that ordinarily to provide the basic human rights of health, literacy, nutrition, clothing, and shelter to a population deprived of them by a small or large ruling class unwilling to expropriate itself in its own long-range best interest, bloody revolutions and the suppression of bourgeois freedoms are necessary. But to denigrate those freedoms is a willful folly equivalent to the assertion that it is not the revolution that sheds blood, but the counterrevolution. It is both, and it is never wise to confuse what is necessary and what is desirable.

Such cauterization of feeling vitiates another, more recent piece on "The Vietnam Wars." That trip to look into the boat people is uncomfortably reminiscent of Naipaul's description of the race of revolutionaries with return air tickets, who, like U.S. politicians in the South Bronx or Sen. Onésimo Sánchez, arrive, make their speeches, and fly away again. The conflicting versions García Márquez had read of the cause of the exodus are reduced at once to the triumphant, vindicatory discovery that the government

5. "The Death of Salvador Allende," trans. Gregory Rabassa, *Harper's*, March 1974, p. 53.

of Vietnam was not in fact "expelling its enemies and forcing them into fatal fishing boats."[6] If ever a straw man limped across a page, that is one. The refugees are divided into collaborators with the old regime, members of the bourgeoisie, and fabulously rich Chinese, who constituted most of the bourgeoisie. There could be no simple people among them, because the terrifying photographs of fugitives arrived in port show that "after several weeks adrift, done in by hunger and the elements and ravaged by pirates, the millionaires of Cholon had become just the same as any poor Chinese" (44). The unfortunate thing about this essay is that García Márquez's premise is correct: Vietnam has been losing the war of information, and its allowing people to leave is as sensible and fundamentally humane as Castro's allowing the various Cuban exoduses. The problem is the inability and the unwillingness of other nations to absorb Vietnam's disaffected. But he misses the opportunity to represent forcefully what emerges almost in spite of him: that Hanoi has not nailed Ho Chi Minh City (Saigon) shut, that considerable freedom of movement and activity exists, that massive efforts to provide social services to the drug addicts, prostitutes, and orphans we left behind have been made with a devastated industrial plant, sterilized agricultural land, and foreign assistance only from the Soviet Union and Sweden, and that there has been no bloodbath. (If there had been, they could not have filled all those boats.) These matters are lost by a point of view that assures us that since the end of the war the North has been working intensely to give back to the South its lost identity, but represents the cultural identity of the North as that of "the small provincial capitals of France" combined with the "four hours of official programs, patriotic documentaries and films from socialist countries" (45) that make up television programming, relieved only by soccer games. In his anxiety to defend Vietnam and his inability not to render precisely what he sees, García Már-

6. "The Vietnam Wars," trans. Gergory Rabassa, *Rolling Stone,* 29 May 1980, pp. 43–46. Although the war with China is mentioned, Vietnam's invasion of Kampuchea is not, another lost opportunity. Vietnam's natural but nasty aspirations to be the regional power in Indochina may be legitimate or illegitimate, but it is hard to disapprove getting rid of the Pol Pot regime by any means available. The failure to mention it, however, looks like deliberate distortion.

quez has wound himself into the for him paradoxical situation of ostensibly praising the life of the North where the city is dead at eight o'clock, melancholy and taciturn, and dispraising the nightlong activity of the city of the South, inverting the long-standing preference in the fiction as elsewhere for the cheerful coast over the gloomy city of the upland north. And in the same way that he disparaged law in the piece on Allende, he here disparages "all the crap for an easy life" still available at inflated prices in Ho Chi Minh City after the war (44).

A different form of this self-compromise in a good cause appears in his self-censorship relative to Cuba. He did not participate in the leftist intellectual protest to Castro on the Heberto Padilla affair because he believed the means ineffective to the end desired but very effective as a tool for those hostile to the revolution. He has expressed reservations about publishing the book on Cuba under the blockade for much the same reason: it contains severe criticisms of errors made by the revolution, and he fears its exploitation by those who do not share his commitment to that revolution in spite of its failures. At the conclusion of his articles on the Cuban airlift to Angola, he asserts that victory in Angola must have provided for the Cubans a long-needed sense of victory after years of unjust reverses and unmerited penances in the deaths of Che and Allende, the U.S. blockade, and "the recondite and implacable moth of so many internal errors of the past that at any moment kept them on the edge of disaster."[7] That awareness of errors is shared by the Cubans in charge, who when the Nicaraguan Sandinistas came seeking advice on what to do, gave them advice on what not to do and provided a list of Cuban actions to avoid. It is probable that García Márquez will lift his self-restraint (he has said the Cubans want him to publish) if we do not see a new wave of right-wing repression in the next decade or if relations between Cuba and the United States are normalized, heads and tails of the same coin.

Although the connections are tenuous, the attitudes described seem to have some bearing on certain formal aspects of García Márquez's fictions, particularly his considered rejection of realistic modes and his habitual man-

7. "Victoria en Angola," *Triunfo* 731 (29 June 1977): 31.

agement of characterization and closure. These three are one: diverse aspects of a radical impatience with the present order of things that suffers from no disillusionment with history because it is confident of the direction in which that history is moving. That impatience appears most clearly in his preference of incisive, schematic renderings of the dynamics of power and oppression to textured social analysis that masks authorial attitudes with full and ostensibly disinterested exposition. Much the same cast of mind is evident in the stylistically parallel characterizations, which are trenchant and decisive, make little use of dialogue to explore the processes of change in characters, and never analyze with intricate delicacy the direction of a glance or the cut of a fingernail. Whether the subject is politics or character, Amaranta's remorse or Sabas's machinations, the effect of García Márquez's method is often brutal as the sentence simultaneously pins down the wriggling object of its contemplation and dismisses it, moving away and on. The direction of that movement is, in turn, never random, though episodic succession and temporal disjunctions may make it seem so. But the proliferation of incident works always to a predetermined and determinate end, however invisible such an end may be either to readers reading or to characters acting or to both at once in Aureliano Babilonia. Insofar as the histories García Márquez records are disillusioning, and they are eminently so, disillusionment is qualified by the revelation that the last things have been foreseen and purposed, whether in the shape of the fiction as a whole or in the deaths of an Arcadio Buendía or an Aureliano José.

There is in García Márquez no covenant with the present or with the past, and the promise of the future is adumbrated only dimly, albeit, when occasion offers, noisily. Such an absence of allegiance would seem to militate against writing fictions at all, as it evidently has not, but it does explicate the curious management of nostalgia in the fictions. With respect to closure, the revolutionary's desire to obliterate the past and present order of things is clear enough. There is a profound impulse to destruction in these fictions, ending so often with an apocalypse, an escape, a wiping away or a wiping clean. Within the fictions, that impulse is countered by the authorial acts of repeating names, characters, and events and hoarding together the accumulated memories of a lifetime, real, imaginary, and literary. Assigned to characters, this alternate tendency becomes the power of nostalgia, that act of the mind that takes us back into the past with a sort of useless yearning. To it, the author attributes great danger. When characters grow nostalgic, they soon die. Or the author kills them, renegades from action to self-consciousness. Fittingly, the fiction in which nostalgia is most prominent is also the most repetitive, the most personal, and the most thorough in its final annihilation. Within the fictions, the two tendencies are held in equilibrium, but putting an end to it all wins out in the end.

The danger nostalgia represents to characters in the fictions is emblematic of García Márquez's vacillation between the traditional humanist distrust of power and the powerful and the realist's knowledge that change can be effected only through the exertion of power by the powerful. Nostalgia is the chief psychological weapon in the arsenal of conservatism, the source of its most effective rhetoric and its hold over the minds of men. As fundamental as memory to the concept of personal identity, nostalgia assures us that the past is not altogether lost, but continuous with the present and the future. Memory tells us this is so, but nostalgia makes us feel it and suggests that we can assuage the pain of loss by embracing it and wrapping ourselves in the faded remnants of the past. If nostalgia suffocates people in the elaborate exorcism of *One Hundred Years of Solitude,* in *The Autumn of the Patriarch* it makes them cling to the dictator. Against the impulse to sustain the past in the present, García Márquez sets the countervailing tendency to break with the past and to begin anew. In common with other apocalypses, his reveals a secret and reinterprets history in the illumination provided by that secret now opened to the initiated. But unlike apocalypses of religious origin, García Márquez's does not describe what lies on the other side of the last things. Nor within the fictions does he name it. If García Márquez's political convictions have the power over him that religious ideas have had over other men, and the extent and nature of his political activities suggest they do, they are revealed in the fictions indirectly, in the bent grasses that show the pressure of the vision. The careful separation he has maintained between his fictions and his polemics and the shift he has made from fiction to polemic intimate that for García Márquez what lies on the other side requires a different, nonfictional genre.

As a politician, García Márquez is less concerned with the happiness of individuals (particularly members of the bourgeoisie, the staple class of fiction) than he is with meliorating the conditions in which people can be unhappy. Unlike some other revolutionarily inclined authors, he does not seem to expect revolutions to emerge from a massive, miraculous change in the consciousness of the people at large, but from the seizure and exertion of power. Revolutions are not born, but made. Among the consequences of such views within the fictions are less interest in the minute analysis of the individual psyche for its own sake than we are accustomed to in much European and North American fiction and no fatuous expectation of a solution to the limitations of human experience through the transformation of the individual. Most of García Márquez's characters, like most people, are happy or unhappy for reasons that have little to do with politics and often little to do even with money, and there do not seem to be any striking solutions proposed to rectify their lives, except for the annihilation of politicians and power, represented by such creatures as Big Mama, the patriarch, and their minions. However considerable the ills inflicted by Big Mama and company, she and her kind do not impinge on everyone all the time, and to obliterate them is only to rid the world of an impediment to people's being as happy as it is possible for them to be. But, as philosophers have long recognized, to be rid of a great evil is not necessarily to possess a great good.

What happiness consists in in positive terms, what might be called García Márquez's social or moral vision, are the simple continuities of ordinary private life: falling in love, raising a family, watching the band on Saturday afternoons in the square, playing checkers, reading books (rarely, except for comic books), doing one's work, going to mass and funerals. These activities are essentially communal, and García Márquez's closest approximation to a value that is individual rather than communal is the intermittent but persistent suggestion that love is redemptive. So attached is he to that notion that, in the face of his own evidence, he uses it to beat the patriarch. Within the fic-

114

tions, the antithesis of love is neither lust nor hatred, but solitude. Both separate the sufferer from a sense of participation in the community, and both are less aspects of character or personality than conditions in which characters find themselves and over which they have no control. Since love and solitude simply happen, there is no rule that can be invoked to enable us to find or escape them, and love itself figures in the fictions much as the imagination does: it changes nothing, but sheds a transforming light over the harsher contours of reality, dissipating, for a moment, the gloom of solitude. It is probably fair to assume that with or without revolution, human beings will continue to suffer requited or unrequited love and that books will be written and read. Like the idea of revolution in the nonfiction, love in the fictions is appealed to as a source of value but never analyzed. That lack of analysis might be objected to as a flaw, but it might also be regarded as a recognition of a mystery far greater than flying carpets, levitations, or sybils' basins.

While a curmudgeon might say that García Márquez's work on behalf of socialism is a fellow-traveling plot to increase world literacy and the sale and serialization of his books so that those poor Vietnamese will no longer have to watch patriotic documentaries on the tube, a fairer view insists that those efforts are motivated by a deep concern for the deprivations most people suffer and by a recognition that changes in that condition will not be made by the goose feather crossed over the kitchen knife, but by the kitchen knife. Meanwhile, the goose feather will do what it can to help, mitigating its powerlessness and solitude through solidarity with a communal vision, in a collective purpose, and returning, revived and reinvigorated, to the liberty of the solitary imagination from its excursions in the world outside the author's study.